LISA SKEFFINGTON

@anxiety

We need to break up

How to get from feeling anxious to empowered in your life.

A fast-track guide for young women.

This book belongs to:

____

@anxiety

We need to break up

Published by Compass-Publishing

ISBN 978-1-912009-25-1

Printed in the UK by CMP UK

Designed by The Book Refinery Ltd.
www.thebookrefinery.com

A catalogue copy of this book is available from the British Library.

Disclaimer

This book isn't intended as a substitute for the medical advice of physicians. The reader should regularly consult a physician in matters relating to his/her health, and particularly with respect to any symptoms that may require diagnosis or medical attention.

I dedicate this book to everyone fighting a secret daily struggle with anxiety, who is feeling trapped in a sense of powerlessness and yet is scared to voice their feelings for fear of ridicule; and to those teenagers who tragically never got the help they needed soon enough to make it all stop.

And if, today, you're feeling such desperation – from my heart to yours – I dedicate my book to you.

Contents

INTRODUCTION 9

STEP 1 - WHAT TO DO TO GET STARTED 13

How to break up with anxiety 15

How to use your breath to relax 25

How to live in the 'now' and take control 29

How to get out of your own way 33

How to quit over thinking 40

How to lower your expectations and give yourself a break 44

STEP 2 - DON'T SWEAT THE SMALL STUFF 49

How to avoid getting overwhelmed 51

How to cope well with exam stress 56

How to heal when your heart breaks 65

How to cope when it feels all too much 70

How to overcome perfectionism 74

How to give your stress and worry away 79

STEP 3 - LEARN TO GET ALONG WITH OTHERS 83

How to bully-proof yourself 85

Contents

How to handle being bullied by a friend or relative 89

How to make friends easily 94

How to avoid getting so worked up 100

How to get them 'off your case' 103

How to be your own best friend 108

STEP 4 - LEARN TO FEEL GOOD ABOUT YOURSELF......113

How to quit pretending and be honest....................115

How to be true to who you are....................119

How to be confident with sex for the first time 124

'Comparanoia' - the fast track to anxiety 129

How to keep your mind healthy....................132

How to feel better about your body 137

STEP 5 - LEARN TO BELIEVE IN YOURSELF 141

How to let your inner confidence shine 143

A square peg in a round hole - the anxiety of not fitting in 147

Contents

Five easy steps to overcome social anxiety........................153

How to overcome the fear of failure..................................158

How to trust yourself in tough times 163

How to stretch and grow...165

NEXT STEPS 169

Unleash your inner warrior..171

RESOURCES 173

REFERENCES 175

MY STORY 176

STUDENT SUCCESS STORIES 178

Introduction

Hey! I'm delighted you've found your way here to me.

I get how frustrating living with anxiety can be. I get how isolated and lost you might feel just now. I know how exhausting it can be to feel on edge, whilst you try to keep your feelings hidden every day. It's hard work trying to pretend you're OK when you're feeling all over the place and you don't even understand why.

I want you to know that it's entirely possible for you to break up with anxiety. Maybe you've tried to get help before, and it didn't work. Don't let anxiety define who you are. The truth is that you just need the right help to know how to take control.

In this fast-track how-to guide, I'm sharing with you some key practical steps to get you on your way, based on my own personal experience. What's more, as I'm an experienced therapist and have been an anxiety expert for a long time now, I've already helped lots of teens just like you.

This book covers what I believe are the key aspects you need to focus on in order to beat anxiety. It's written in a flexible way that makes it easy for you to use it as a quick guide whenever you need help with a specific challenge. It's not essential to read it through from start to finish. You can simply go to what speaks to you first, or choose to dip in and out of the different strategies as and when you need to.

I'd recommend that you jot down and practise the strategies that speak to you the most. It's a great idea to buy a journal and write about how you feel as you try out the strategies I'll be sharing with you. Journaling is a fantastic and private means to help you to understand yourself more, as you will become more aware of your thoughts and emotions. Alternatively, you might like to use the notes sections throughout the book.

I know for myself that it can be tough, for girls especially, finding your way through the teenage years. As a girl, you'll tend to suffer more than a boy because you deal with stress by focusing your attention inside yourself, overthinking and over-feeling everything, don't you? (This isn't always the case, but I find it is most times.) Whereas, a boy will typically deal with stress by focusing outside himself and getting physical. Boys are just more wired to take action that way. It's really common for healthy teenage girls to develop anxiety. This can be due to hormonal fluctuations, the struggles of developing an identity, steering your way through first relationships and managing friendship fall-outs, amongst other reasons. I had anxiety myself as a teenager, and I've helped professionally many young women ease their anxiety by using the strategies in this book. It's not always possible for everyone to consult directly with me, but I didn't want you to miss out on getting vital help for yourself at this difficult time. This is why I've written this book for you.

Oh, by the way, it's OK to share this book with your parent(s) or guardian(s), because – you know what – they may secretly need the same help too! It may provide you with the opportunity to be more honest and open with each other when you start talking about how you really feel.

Throughout the book, I've included links to further resources. I highly recommend that you take every offer of support that I give you. I'm hoping my book will help you to find the hope and the positivity that you need. I want you to understand what's possible. I want you to find your courage to take action as you need to.

There's so much you can do to get rid of anxiety, so that you can feel better about yourself and within yourself in every way. You're already amazing, and I'm going to prove it to you.

I'm sure you're keen to get started, so let's get on with it!

Step 1

What to do to get started

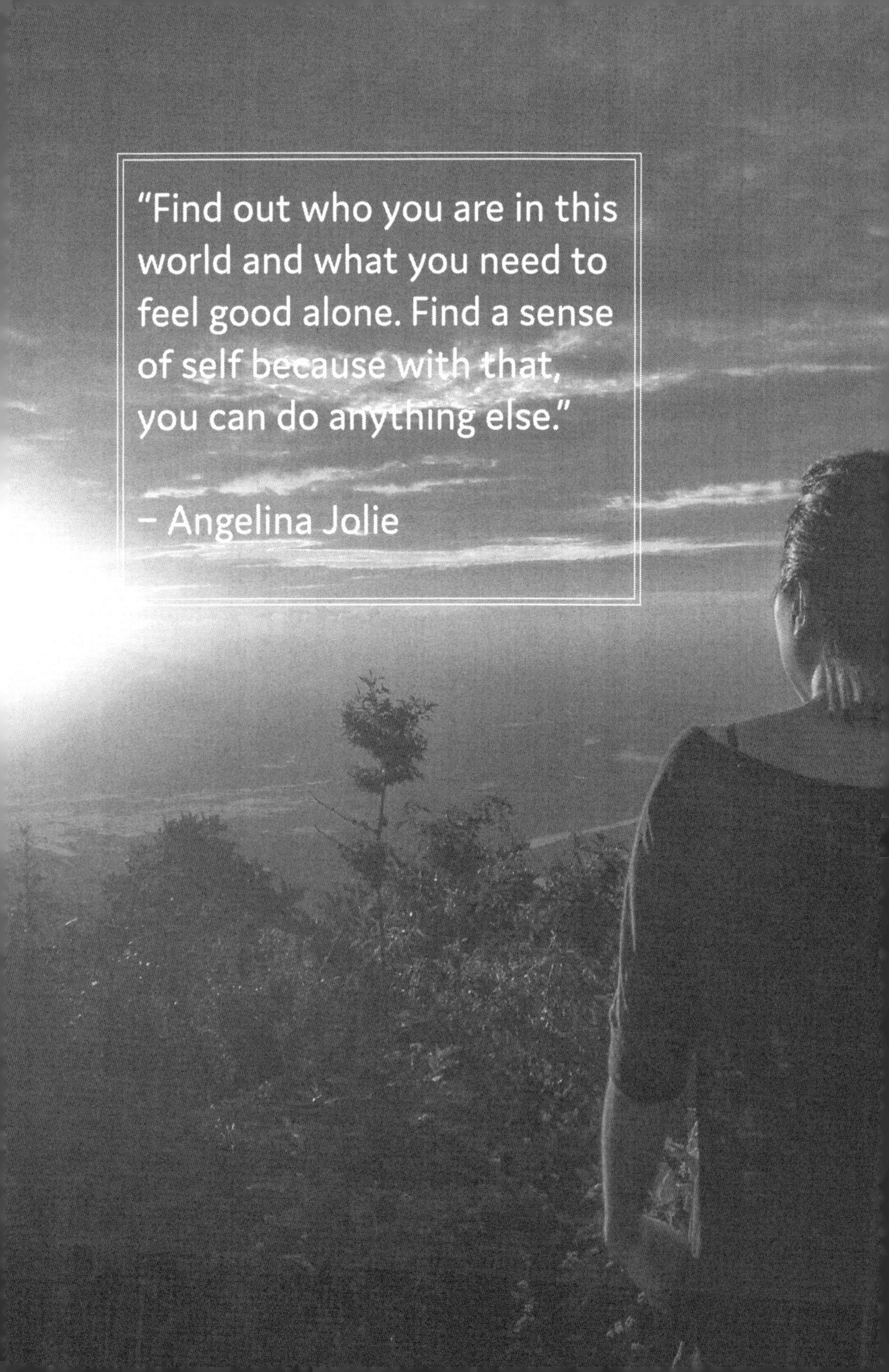
"Find out who you are in this world and what you need to feel good alone. Find a sense of self because with that, you can do anything else."
– Angelina Jolie

How to break up with anxiety

First of all, you must know that generalised anxiety is really like a friend you can do without. It's time to break up, and I'm going to help you.

Secondly, it's a great idea to get a real understanding of where you are with anxiety. I'd recommend that you spend a few minutes to take my *online anxiety quiz*. It'll help you to gauge the full impact of how anxiety is screwing things up for you just now. You'll find a resources page at the back of the book, but to access this right now go to www.anxietybreakup.com/resources.

Mind your language!

When students come to see me, they typically talk about 'my anxiety' or 'my illness', saying things such as "Because of my anxiety", "It's my anxiety that gets in the way", "Ever since I've had my illness" and so on.

When you take possession of it, it becomes yours. It becomes part of who you are: a part of your identity. Don't you think that, if your subconscious identifies you as *entwined* with anxiety, it would make it more difficult to get rid of for yourself, rather than it just being something you're experiencing right now?

How did you come to own 'your' anxiety?

Essentially, you absorb thoughts and ideas from others; if you're told them often enough or if certain events happen often enough, these ideas become fact, and an expectation is created within you. This is a process of direct control. If you're repeatedly told "If you do x, then y will happen", then – over time – you begin to believe it.

These are things such as "If you run, you'll fall over", "If you speak up, people will laugh at you or they won't like you", "If you get it wrong, you'll look stupid" or "If you try, you'll fail".

In a process of indirect control, what you tell yourself about what others say to you or how they behave towards you determines a set of beliefs you grow to live by.

So, you might tell yourself things such as "I can't run safely", "I'm always falling over", "I don't know what I'm talking about", "Everyone's ready to find a reason not to like me", "I'm so stupid", "I always get it wrong" or "I can't do it".

Do you get the idea?

When the combination of these ideas appears remarkably different from what you want for yourself or what you know to be fundamentally true about yourself, this creates a conflict within you. You want to do something, be someone or have something in your life, but another part of you is telling you that you can't, as it doesn't fit with what your identity or what your 'life script' says about you. (Your life script is like a personal list of beliefs that you live your life by.) This means that a struggle within your nervous system begins and anxiety is the result.

In many circumstances, certain beliefs about who you are and what you're able to do may be out of date, and not fit with your current circumstances. Often, what you were told in the past was a judgement based on someone else's subconscious, limiting beliefs. You might ask yourself the following: "Is that belief correct?", "Am I right to hold that belief?", "Who says they were right?" or "What do they really know?"

Whatever it was, after all, it was just their idea, their opinion from their own world view and their experience. Just because your mind and body have, in the past, created a certain way of seeing the world, the past doesn't equal the future – *you have a choice in that*. Perceived or real past circumstances, which were perhaps threatening or frightening in the past, are only kept alive in the present by your thoughts and feelings about those past times.

The best way to help yourself is to focus your attention fully in the present moment. This is called 'grounding yourself'. Then, tell yourself, "That was *then*, this is *now!*" The past is gone. It's simply your thoughts that keep it real for you now.

When you aren't grounded in the present, you'll find that, by association, similar events recreate past fears. When this keeps happening, you make those fears real for yourself in the present. You bring those past fears into your present reality – that's what you do, right?

When you think about meeting new people or doing something outside your comfort zone, those doubts about yourself and your abilities bubble up, as your mind and body remember how you responded in the past to similar stimuli, and you own the anxious feelings because you believe that's who you are.

Here's the good news. *You don't have to own those past fears in the present.* That recurring anxious feeling does *not* mean it's now part of you. Unless, of course, you choose for it to be. It's just a feeling that's coming up as a result of self-limiting beliefs, based on a past learned behavioural response. You can't easily chop off your ear or your arm – your subconscious just wouldn't let you – at least, not without a great deal of pain and you would probably pass out in the process! This all sounds a bit dramatic, but the truth is that the same idea applies to anxiety when you make it yours.

A student was explaining her struggle with moving on from anxiety and depression, which had coloured her life for many years. As she was talking, she said, "You see, because of my anxiety…", and then later she said, "It makes it easier for my depression to come back…" When I pointed out to her how, by the use of her language, she was taking possession of that anxiety and depression, she laughed saying, "It's like a teddy bear that I carry around with me and don't want to let go!" It does become a comfort, and it can have hidden benefits or gains attached, which you might not realise or even own up to.

Your mind takes possession so seriously that it becomes an instruction to make anxiety and depression part of who you are. It's almost as if it becomes a ball and chain you wear. This ball and chain limits you in terms of what you can do and who you can be. It's a ball and chain that others pick up from you in your energy, in how you come across and in your body language, and also in your thoughts – both in how you talk to yourself (called self-talk) and in how you talk to others. You *will* find yourself tied to the restrictions of anxiety. It determines how others view you consciously and subconsciously, what others expect of you, and what you expect of yourself.

So don't own it! If you own it, you'll always be anxious or depressed. Your mind will see to that. What I'm saying here is this: *mind your language!* Don't own something you don't want. If you don't own anxiety, you'll make it possible for you to break yourself free from it.

Action point: Make it happen!

My online series *The No. 1 Secret to Overcoming Anxiety* provides a workbook to help you further with this point. For some extra hands-on support, to get yourself off to a flying start, see the resources section at the back of this book or go directly to www.anxietybreakup.com/resources.

Stop fuelling anxiety with those what-if catastrophes

If you tend to think negatively and struggle with anxiety, it's likely that you're negatively programming yourself and making your anxiety symptoms worse.

When you think negatively about any situation and when you begin to imagine those endless, worrying what-if scenarios – which feed anxiety – have you noticed that your mind constructs negative pictures in line with those negative thoughts?

To the subconscious mind, imagination is reality. This makes something you fear will happen actually appear real. The subconscious mind works effectively with images. It has poor logical and rational capabilities – that's a job for the conscious mind. It doesn't know the difference between imagined and real.

Imagine you're sucking on a lemon or an onion – it doesn't have a great taste, does it? Alternatively, imagine standing on the edge of a very high building with your toes off the edge, and – with the slightest shift in balance – you'll easily fall; do you feel yourself pull back? Your mind is tricking your body into believing something is happening, and your body responds sharply, and yet your conscious mind knows it isn't really happening at all. Nightmares and anxiety work in the same way.

By programming (also known as hypnotising) yourself with these uncomfortable pictures, it creates a belief that your fears are actually already happening. Your body responds by flooding itself with the stress hormones of adrenalin and cortisol to combat a perceived threat, albeit an imagined one. If the subconscious perceives this as real, by your negative thoughts and imaginings, you're hypnotising yourself into creating programmes of negative expectations.

When you find yourself in similar situations to those you fear and have already experienced dramatic consequences to in your imagination, the anxiety response is more intense because the subconscious believes you're facing that imagined traumatic and disastrous situation once more – and it knows the negative extent of what happened last time because it was your worst fear played out!

As with an iceberg, the majority of the mind's force is concealed below the surface of your conscious daily awareness, and this deeper subconscious function controls your urges, reflexes, gut reactions, irrational fears and habitual behaviour. It wants you to avoid repeating that dreadful scenario at all costs. This heightens your anxiety and spirals you deeper into the anxiety trap.

FIND YOUR POWER!

So, if the mind is so skilled at combining thoughts and images to create an intense feeling and a perceived outcome that appears real, are you perhaps wondering, "Wouldn't it be great to learn how to harness that skill in a positive way?"

Just imagine how you might befriend your mind and begin to unlock your own power within. If you hold the power to hypnotise yourself negatively into a frenzy, couldn't you use that same power in a different and better way, and set yourself free?

What if you could set yourself free from anxiety and achieve whatever you want to achieve?

Here's how you can get started...

» Take a few moments to just sit quietly and begin to imagine, in as much detail as you can, just how you want yourself and your life to be. Imagine that you wake-up tomorrow morning and things have become exactly how you wished they could be.

» Pay attention to what's different, and how and why you feel differently within yourself.

» Positively imagine and visualise how you want to be and feel within yourself, and you'll set a programme

in motion within your subconscious mind to help you get there.

» Challenge every catastrophising what-if thought with a "So what if…", and get creative with how you'll cope if the worst happens. When you trust that you can handle any confidence crisis, you'll feel more empowered to live your life on your terms.

» As you learn to break up with anxiety, the strategies that follow in this book will help you to feel happier and more in control. This quotation really motivated me to find a way to overcome anxiety for myself. I'd read it aloud to myself, and dare to imagine a life feeling free and secure within myself, as I am now.

"*… and then one day the risk to remain tight in a bud was more painful than the risk it took to blossom.*" – Anaïs Nin

» All the strategies I'm about to share with you will help you to look at the anxiety you're experiencing in a different way. As you choose to adopt these strategies in your day-to-day life, like adding droplets of water into a glass, you'll notice how you'll be feeling calmer and stronger. You'll begin to 'unfriend' anxiety and distance yourself from it. This will help you to feel more powerful and in control, not just of yourself but of your life too. I've presented this book in a way that makes it easy for you to find any strategy you need reminding of, in a simple and straightforward way.

» I've included some extra resources at the back of this book to help you further.

Take it one day at a time, and always remember that if I can do it, you can too!

Notes:

How to use your breath to relax

When you focus on breathing the right way, you challenge your body's stress response and help your body get yourself back in balance.

In today's busy world, most people are running on adrenalin and are therefore breathing in a shallow way into their chest. I wonder how you breathe?

You can test it now by doing the following.

» Place one hand on your chest and one hand on your tummy. Breathe in and then breathe out. Which hand is moving more?

» Do it again and breathe more deeply. Notice again which hand moves more.

» If it's your chest hand, you're in fight-or-flight mode and running with some degree of background stress.

Unless you're feeling particularly stressed at this moment, this is how you tend to breathe. This means that it's become a habit for you to breathe in this shallow way, which is depriving your body of vital oxygen and nutrients, and fuelling the physiological stress response.

Action point: Make it happen!

Learning how to breathe for balance is so vital to your wellbeing. I really do want you to get to grips with this. I've created an infographic flow diagram for you, to walk you through the steps. See the resources page at the back of the book, or got directly to www.anxietybreakup.com/resources.

FIND YOUR POWER!

Here's how to retrain your body to breathe correctly:

- Again, place one of your hands on your chest and the other on your tummy.
- This time, imagine that there's a deflated balloon in your tummy. Imagine what colour it is.
- Now, as you breathe in through your nose, direct your breath right down to your diaphragm, where it meets your stomach. As you do this, imagine the balloon inflating and picture how its colour spreads. Gently lift your hand a little off your tummy to encourage your tummy to follow your hand up.
- Then, breathe out through your mouth, pressing your tummy hand flat into your stomach, and deflate the balloon.
- Repeat this exercise until you get the hang of it. If you've been breathing into your chest for some time, it may take you a little effort to get your breathing back in sync. Stay with it.
- Aim to breathe in for a count of four, hold it for two whilst you focus on the colour and contours of the

inflated balloon, and then breathe out for eight. You can build up to this, of course. Begin with two–one–four then increase to three–two–six.

» The more you practise this, the more relaxed you'll feel.

This style of breathing is called *tummy breathing*.

With practise, as soon as you catch yourself getting stressed and become aware that you're breathing into your chest, you can ward off an adrenalin rush by directing your breath down to your stomach. The automatic stress response will begin to ease, and you'll feel calmer and more balanced in your physiology.

With the spiralling anxiety I suffered for many years, I had got into the habit of breathing incorrectly since childhood. When I realised – as an adult – that my breath was fuelling my anxiety response, I set about changing it, and it was a huge step in my recovery towards achieving balance and wellbeing.

Aim to practise this ten times in the morning, at midday and in the evening. It really works when you get the hang of it! And you'll be able to help yourself effectively when you need it most.

Notes:

How to live in the 'now' and take control

If you're living with anxiety day to day, I wonder how in control of your thoughts you feel? From my personal encounters with anxiety, I remember how all I wanted in any one moment of anxiety was to stop my thoughts leaping and spiralling.

Perhaps you feel the same?

When this happens, it's difficult to keep your attention focused on now. Your mind floods with self-doubt and fear, and you search frantically for an answer based on how you handled something in the past. Your mind operates this way because it's using past experiences to try to find out how you might help yourself right now, but your mind's already racing into the future, fearing all the what-if scenarios that your very active imagination is creating.

So, how can you help yourself to be more in the present and calm your anxiety?

The trick is to learn some strategies to ground yourself in the present time.

FIND YOUR POWER!

You must learn to keep your focus in the present moment.

Here's how:

- Make sure both your feet are on the floor. This will instantly help to stabilise you. You can even get your mind's attention by stamping your feet on the ground. This will interrupt your train of thought and make you clearly aware that your feet are in contact with the ground in that moment. Say to yourself, "Back to *now!*" to interrupt your thinking every time you catch your mind wandering off into the past or into the future.
- Focus on your breathing. Your breathing is happening right now. Notice how, when you feel anxious, your breathing is very shallow and quicker. You breathe from your chest when you're experiencing a fight-or-flight response. Channel your breath further down to your diaphragm by practising tummy breathing, which is where each breath you take goes deep into your body and inflates your tummy, rather than inflating your chest. Follow your breath as you breathe in for a count of three, inflating your

tummy for two, and deflate it as you breathe out for a count of six.

» Use your senses to really tune in to how you're experiencing your surroundings. Take a moment to really focus on each of your senses (touch, taste, smell, hearing and sight), which will bring your awareness onto your immediate environment. Focus on the details you see in the room you're in or on the details of the furnishings; the sounds you hear around you, such as people chatting, the music playing or the cars whizzing by; the taste of anything you're eating; the smell of the air; or even how it feels to be sitting in the chair you're in or how your feet feel inside your shoes as you walk. You get the idea.

» Own your feelings in the present moment by saying to yourself something like, "Right now, I'm feeling upset, and what I really need right now is to go for a walk, to get a glass of water or to ground myself."

» Choose to tell yourself something (anything) positive in that moment. This is called an affirmation. Begin this with the words, "Right now, I am..."

  You can use affirmations such as, "Right now, I'm learning to create new ways to feel better about myself," or "Right now, I'm focusing on keeping my attention where it needs to be."

» Remind yourself that the past is over and whatever happened then isn't happening now.

- » Realise that, by worrying about the future, you're simply creating an expectation in your mind based on fear. You're effectively creating a movie in your mind and scaring yourself, but it isn't real. Instead, choose to give your mind more positive expectations by creating a nicer picture, which you can anticipate in a more positive and happier way.
- » Remember that your power is always in the present moment.

Learn to direct your mind to be on the present, and you'll begin to feel more powerful within your own mind.

Notes:

How to get out of your own way

Have you ever really wanted to do something for yourself or make a change in your circumstances for the better, only to then sabotage your attempts to give yourself a break? Maybe you feel frustrated and powerless that you just can't seem to make it happen?

Here's what you need to remember when it all feels like too much. It's subconscious programming buried deeply within your mind that triggers such resistance. This 'pull back to comfort' might feel like an anxious or stuck feeling. It feels very strong. It's an instinctive response from the subconscious to steer you away from the possible threat of unknown territory and back into the perceived safety of the familiar.

FIND YOUR POWER!

There are steps you can take to help you create the change you want to see in your life more easily and more quickly.

Here are my suggestions for keeping anxiety under control and getting you on track for success:

1. **Own the problem.** The first critical step in breaking free from anxiety is to accept that it's the way you're thinking or behaving in your life that's getting in your own way of creating the change you want to see. You can't control your circumstances, but you can learn to respond and react in a different way that's more helpful to you.
2. **Take responsibility** for the stress that's showing up in your life and accept that *only you* can make a change happen. In the same way, a personal trainer can't do your sit-ups for you. You go to the gym and you put the commitment in to see results. When you're proactive and you take responsibility, you empower yourself to create success in your life and keep it going.
3. **Be patient.** Whilst – without doubt – you'll get flashes of inspiration and enlightenment, shifts in perspective, or even giant leaps in

awareness, transformation is a process of growing to become your best self. You must give it time for sustained improvement to be long lasting. You need to develop awareness, so that you can take action in the form of the critical steps needed to integrate this awareness into your daily living.

4. **Learn to visualise.** You need to know how to create change for yourself, step by step, in a comfortable way. Visualisation is one effective brain-training strategy that can create change more easily and quickly. If you fear failing, for example, this idea can really help to calm performance anxiety and can be particularly helpful with exam stress.

» When you invest in spending a short time every day to visualise yourself overcoming particular fears or behaviours (which is also called 'pre-play'), it creates an illusion in your mind that you're experiencing it for real, yet in a totally safe and comfortable way. The more feeling you put into it and the more you engage your senses in the experience, the deeper the effect. This is because you're engaging the neural pathways effectively within your brain. In order to create long-lasting change, you must actively reconfigure your neural pathways. When you relax and imagine things going well for you, the old, 'wired-into-your-brain' fear programming gets overwritten by a more comfortable idea. The more you do this consistently, the more familiar and comfortable the imagined experience becomes, simply because you get more comfortable in your 'stretch zone'. When you're in your stretch zone, you're doing things that are stretching you beyond what feels comfortable and familiar to you. This creates a shift in real-life situations, because the old, wired-in subconscious response has been overwritten.

5. **Take action to keep moving forwards.** At times, when you pull back inside your safe comfort zone, please understand how you're feeding the anxiety you want to get rid of. Fear doesn't stop you moving forwards; only you do that!
6. **You either win or you learn.** You never win or lose in life. You only lose when you quit. Learning comes from experience and careful reflection, so that you can begin to understand how you can get better and stronger, and why things didn't work out this time.
7. **Nothing will change unless you take the right action.** Realise that, unless you do something different in your thinking and in your actions, you'll continue to get the same outcomes in your life. As Einstein is often suggested to have said (though there's no proof he actually did), "The definition of insanity is doing the same thing over and over and expecting different results."

Facing your fears and 'slaying that dragon' can be challenging. Growing to become your best self is a process, and it can feel confusing. The moment when you may falter is the very moment when you're nearest to a breakthrough, so hang in there! After all, it's unlikely you'll learn to ride a horse without falling off a few times.

The magic happens when you muster the courage and the determination to get back on the horse and reset yourself.

Notes:

How to quit over thinking

When you worry about something, how many times do you think the same worrying thought, I wonder? Do you ever catch yourself going over and over that worrying thought to the point where it feels like a cyclone sucking you in that you just can't escape? You try to think about something else, but your mind just comes back to that worrying thought.

This process of going over and over a pattern of thinking in your mind is called 'rumination' – it's a great word, don't you think?

You might even feel frustrated with yourself that you keep tormenting or perhaps frightening yourself in this way, where your mood spirals downwards, and yet you still keep going over those same worries. When this happens, it may feel as if you're letting your thoughts take control.

How to stop

The key is to retrain your mind to break the habit by distracting yourself. Busy yourself in a different way. Break the pattern of your thoughts by giving your mind something else to focus on. That worrying thought just fills a moment, and if you're filling that moment with something else – with some other action or thought – there's no opportunity for that worrying thought to come through.

You'll begin to interrupt the pattern by inhibiting or stopping the worrying thought from resurfacing.

FIND YOUR POWER!

Think about how you might distract yourself – just to fill those few moments and to distract yourself for a few moments at a time.

Get busy. Take some positive, proactive action to keep you occupied and focused on something practical.

Here are some examples:

- Tidy up your room or any cupboards, or sort through your wardrobe.
- Sing a few lines of a favourite song.
- Count backwards from a random high number.
- Change your position – which is an excellent way to interrupt a chain of thought – so if you're sitting, stand up and move.
- Read something backwards.
- Notice the detail of something particular in your environment.
- Tune into your senses, and notice what you see, hear, taste, smell and touch.
- Follow your breath, especially your out-breath.

Do anything that gets your thinking away from that worrying thought or idea, and takes you to a better and calmer place within yourself. You'll begin to distance yourself from those worries, which helps you to gain some perspective and calm your reactions to the fears you're imagining.

When you're slightly calmer, ask yourself, "Is this is a rational or irrational worry [i.e. does it make sense to worry about this]? Is there some action I can take right now to ease this worry and get some certainty on a situation I'm unsure about?" If there is, then go perform the action, make the call, or go meet that particular someone and have the conversation.

Action point: Make it happen!

I've created a great checklist to help you further with this, called *Top Ten Tips to Manage Irrational Thoughts.* It's listed on the resources page at the back of the book, but to access this right now the link is www.anxietybreakup.com/resources.

Notes:

How to lower your expectations and give yourself a break

Are you perhaps tired of feeling overwhelmed, always on the go and in a hurry?

If this is you, then you may need to create some space around you, mentally and physically. It might be a good idea for you to simplify things in your environment, in your friendships and relationships, and in your life in general.

The biggest reason life gets complicated is from expecting too much of yourself and from being too hard on yourself.

FIND YOUR POWER!

Let's look at what you might do to be kind to yourself in ten easy steps:

1. Get some regular downtime away from technology, social media and television – you'll be amazed how much time you'll create.
2. Be content with less. Clear out your clutter. Moderation is the key in every area of your life, not just materially but physically and psychologically too. Less in some areas creates space to do more in other areas, so – overall – your life will become more balanced.

3. Reduce the drama. Let daily niggles pass you by and go over your head. You know the saying – "Don't sweat the small stuff."
4. Take yourself outdoors and get some physical exercise. Simply walking boosts your energy and inspires creativity.
5. Don't take yourself too seriously and learn to laugh at yourself.
6. Take responsibility for the circumstances you find yourself in and the actions you choose to take. Quit blaming others and complaining.
7. Accept that you aren't superhuman. It's OK to mess up sometimes. You can't

stay on top of everything all the time. Learn to accept that there are times when you can't do it all alone, and allow yourself to ask for support when you need it.

8. Forgive yourself when you make mistakes, and forgive others for their mistakes too. Otherwise, the only one you ultimately punish is yourself.
9. Don't worry so much about other people's agendas: what they said, what they did or how they might judge you. Adopt the belief that most people are well intentioned and are trying to do the best they can with what they know right now. They can do no more, and neither can you.
10. Let go of perfection. Simply strive to be the best you can be instead.

Notes:

Step 2

Don't sweat the small stuff

Calm is your superpower

How to avoid getting overwhelmed

Do you feel sometimes that your life is so busy that you almost don't have time to have a wobble? Maybe you find yourself so caught up in everyday human 'doing' that you end up stressed out, uptight and wondering what it's all about? Things can spiral out of control as stress mounts during a typical day, so you may notice yourself getting wound tighter and tighter in your chest or your stomach.

In these times, you'll be running on adrenalin, in what's known as fight-or-flight mode. This is the instinctive response to stress, which cavemen experienced in order to be able to stand and fight, or run away fast. Today, it's common to function in some degree of fight-or-flight mode just to cope with the demands on you in everyday life.

FIND YOUR POWER!

Remember that you're a human 'being' first, so allow yourself to just be. Try to find some time in your day when you can pay attention to your breathing, and when you can get outside and reconnect with the nature around you. Schedule the time as if it were a vitally important appointment that you simply can't miss. I guarantee you that it'll help you to regain a sense of perspective on your day. Your intuition, creativity and even your memory are stifled by stress – so do yourself a favour and schedule some quiet time into your day to reconnect with your still, calm voice inside. This voice (your intuition) knows just what needs to happen and just what you need to do.

This sense of 'inner knowing' is your guide, if only you'll be still and quiet enough to listen.

Here are a few ideas:

» If you live in the city, find a park to walk in or a river to walk by.

» Even if you can't get out for some reason, play your favourite soothing music, using headphones, and escape for a short time.

» If you're lucky enough to live near a forest or the coast, take yourself there, breathe the fresh air and enjoy the space around you.

- Lose yourself in having fun with your friends or playing with your pet.
- Go for a swim in a pool, or – better still – if you can, swim outdoors in the sea or in a lake.
- Do something that engages your mind in a completely different way, such as a conundrum, a crossword puzzle or some kind of art.
- Watch some comedy sketches.

Your body and your mind will thank you by giving you better health, sharper thinking and calmer nerves.

Action point: Make it happen!

You can get access to my free audio download, which will help you to shift perspective and de-stress in ten minutes. I'll guide you through offloading any emotional burdens you may be feeling, as you imagine walking together with me along the seashore. It's listed on the resources page at the back of the book, but to access this right now the link is www.anxietybreakup.com/resources.

Notes:

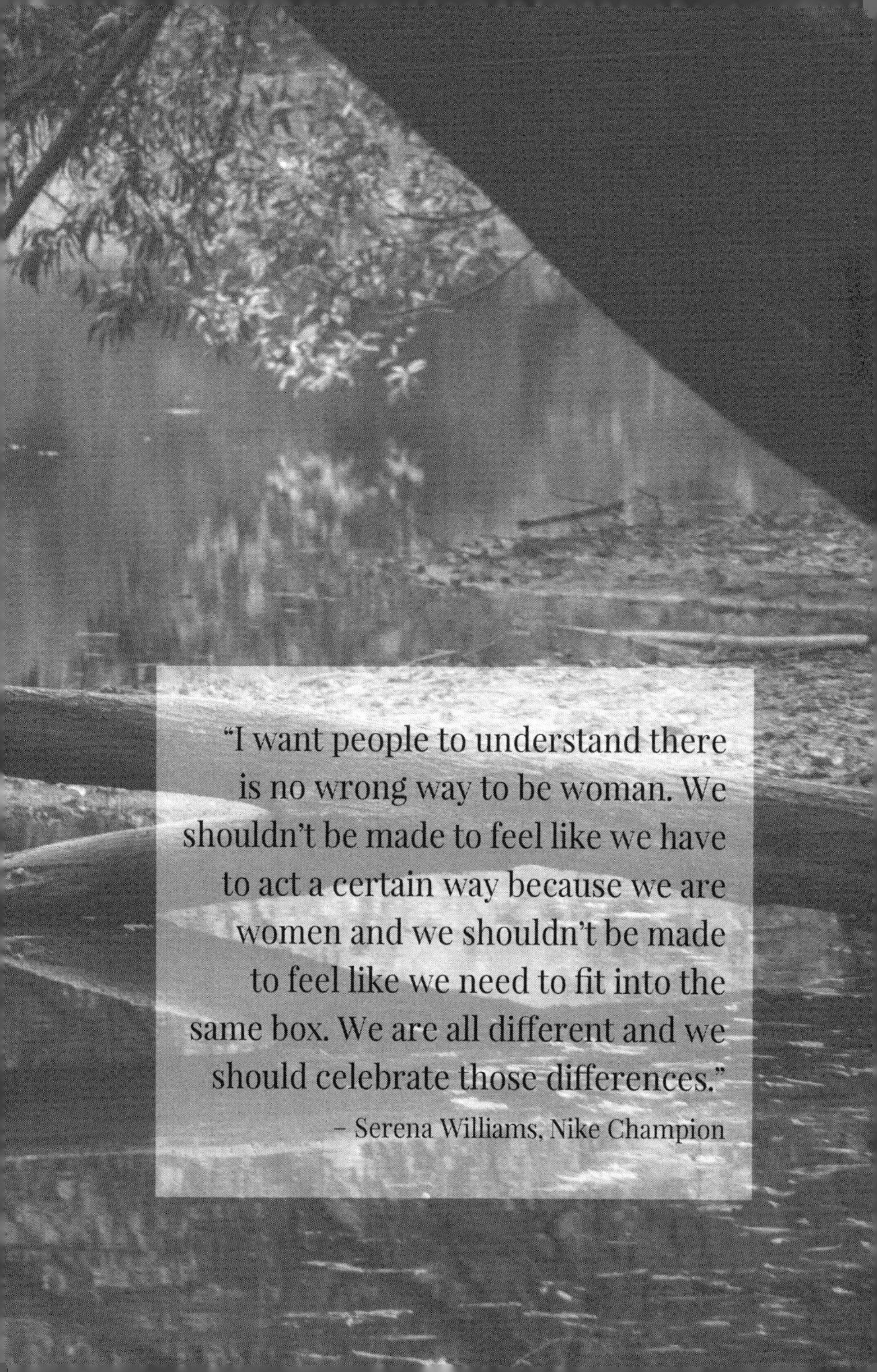
"I want people to understand there is no wrong way to be woman. We shouldn't be made to feel like we have to act a certain way because we are women and we shouldn't be made to feel like we need to fit into the same box. We are all different and we should celebrate those differences."
– Serena Williams, Nike Champion

How to cope well with exam stress

An exam of any kind can cause huge stress. It throws up a fear of failing, but – more than that – it causes you to doubt yourself and your ability to perform when you really have to. It's normal to feel apprehensive of any exam because it's an unknown. The truth is that you don't know what the questions will be or what specifically will be required of you until that moment when you suddenly have to pull it out of the bag and *perform*. If you feel under pressure to perform well in your exams, you're not alone. The repercussions of falling short in any performance – whether it's sport related or academic – can feel overwhelming, can't they?

I wonder if you understand what's underneath your fears? It's worthwhile asking yourself some probing questions, so that you understand what it is you're really worried about.

Exam stress brings with it the pressure of not wanting to let your parents/guardians or teachers/lecturers down. Go deeper and confront what you fear might happen if you do let them down. Do you worry that your parents' love or your teachers' respect only hinges on you being good enough to pass your exams? Being brave enough to confront these mostly inaccurate worries, with some honest conversations with your parents or teachers, will – in most cases – diffuse a lot of angst and help you to go into the exam feeling more at ease.

If your self-esteem or self-confidence is shaky, perhaps you're worrying about the humiliation if your friends pass, but you don't. Perhaps, in some circumstances, it's that you'll be moved down and you won't be with your friends. Working on how you feel about yourself will help you to worry less and get your focus back on your studying. Keep reading and you'll get some fantastic strategies that'll show you how to do this.

FIND YOUR POWER!

Here's a simple strategy to get you in the right mindset for success!

It's vital that you plan and invest in study time. *Anxiety feeds on a lack of preparation*. Set yourself a realistic timetable, weeks ahead of the exam(s). List all the areas of study required and the time you calculate you'll need for each area. Be realistic and be sure to break it down into bite-sized chunks of study. Be sure to tick off the study you've done as you complete it, so that you can clearly remind yourself how well you're on track with revision, when you have a wobble.

Decide on the study methods that suit you best, and invest in any materials you may need to complete your revision.

Imagine your mind is like a memory bank, storing away information in the right files/folders within your subconscious mind. Imagine that – as you're reading, writing or typing – the information is flowing through what I like to call the 'information superhighways'. Think of them as information channels. Your brain is made of thousands of networks and is able to transmit a vast amount of information rapidly (just like the internet, which was referred to as an information superhighway in the past).

Imagine seeing this stored information. It can help to imagine it in a tangible form, such as a coloured liquid in a clear memory tank or colour-coded files of information within the extensive library of your mind.

Tell yourself, as you study, that you're absorbing everything you need to know and that the information is safely there for when you'll need to recall it, just like taking a book off a shelf or opening a computer file.

Once you're into a good study routine, then you can begin to imagine yourself in the exam itself. Imagine yourself there, trusting that you have all the information you need with you and all you have to do is to send a signal to your subconscious that you're ready for the information to flow in reverse along that information superhighway.

Visualise yourself there in the exam, with the information flowing as you answer the questions and do what's required to complete the exam. As you rehearse your success, imagine that your thoughts are really positive and encouraging, helping you to feel calm and relaxed as you steadily complete the exam. Imagine what you'll tell yourself, and how you'll be thinking in a light and upbeat way.

Then, imagine the feeling of leaving the exam hall, knowing that you did your best, and that the time you invested in absorbing and storing away the information was so worthwhile.

Remember that confidence isn't something you have, being confident is something you do; the more you rehearse how your mind experiences success, the more your feelings of confidence and calm will grow.

Action point: Make it happen!

I've helped many students to overcome exam stress by following this framework. At the back of this book is a resource section where you'll find details of how to work with me directly if you need more in-depth help. As well as one-to-one help, there's an option for you to come on board with me through a six-week online mentoring programme. During this, we'll dive into deeper strategies to help you develop your confidence, academically and socially, with plenty of opportunity for questions and answers too. The link to find out more is www.anxietybreakup.com/resources.

Notes:

Notes:

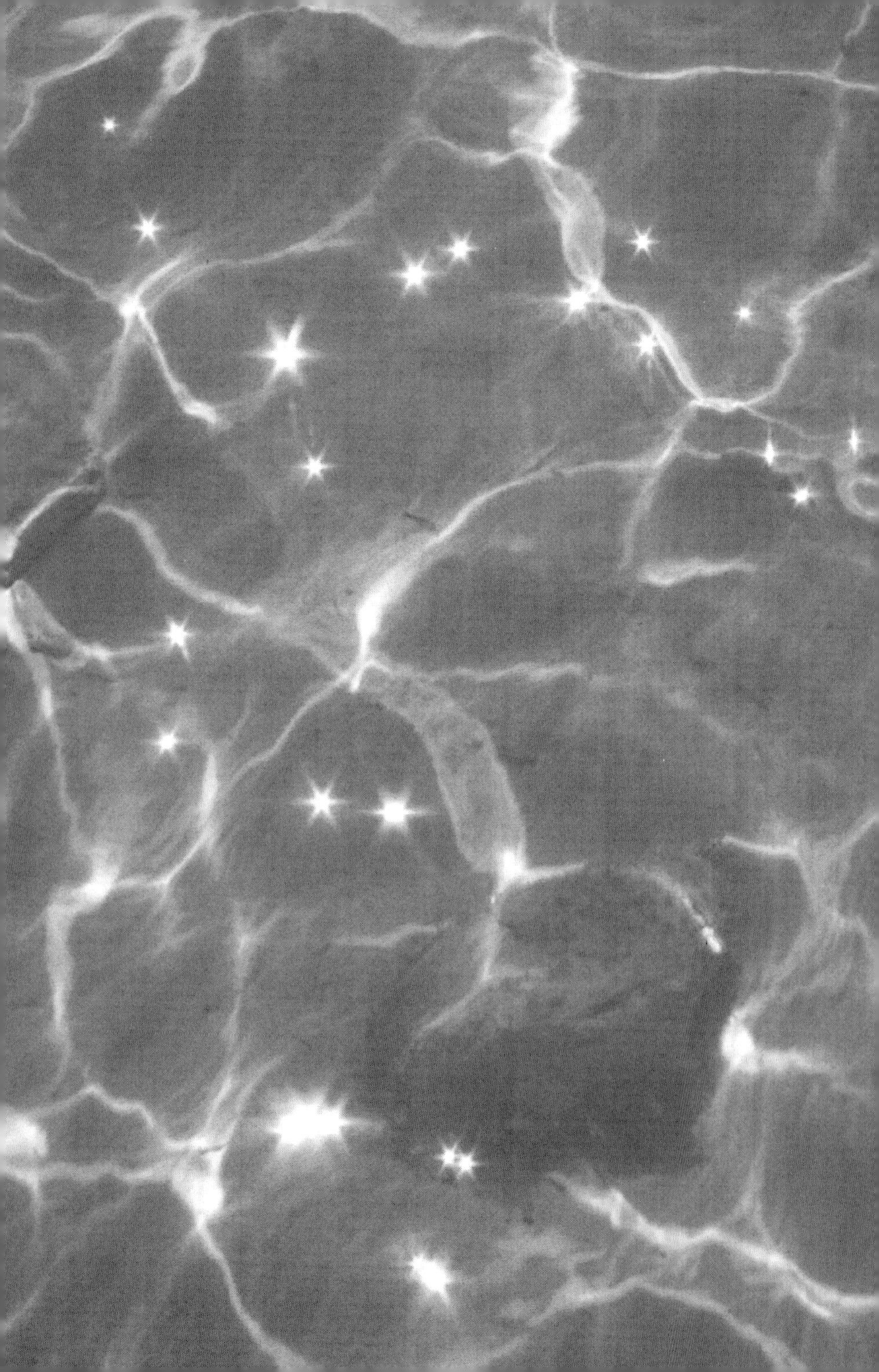

How to heal when your heart breaks

Sometimes, when heartbreak happens in a way you never saw coming, it's a bit like a meteor crashing down from outer space. One minute you're feeling really happy and the world is a wonderful place, and then – out of the blue – you get dumped. You didn't see it coming, and it's horrid. Shock can send your emotions reeling, and you might feel as if you're losing control or are even disconnected from reality for a short time.

When this happens to you (as it inevitably does to us all at some time), I want you to follow my steps here to help you get a grip on your emotions, so that you can start to move yourself steadily through your heartbreak.

FIND YOUR POWER!

Firstly, you need to accept that your emotions are disrupted and your body may be reacting with physical distress reactions, such as shallow breathing that's quicker than normal, difficulty sleeping or an upset tummy. You'll likely experience symptoms of high anxiety and perhaps even panic attacks. For a short time, this is normal.

If you think you might be in emotional shock, in that moment, try to eat and drink something sweet. When adrenalin rises, blood-sugar levels can plummet, so something sweet can help the body to regain its balance.

It can take a little time for the reality of the situation to kick in, and you might not cry straight away. As the shock begins to wear off, you'll feel very sad, so get ready for a flood of tears! Don't hold back. Tears are a normal reaction to sudden loss and emotional pain.

You can't help but feel rejected when someone makes it clear they don't want to be with you anymore, and – trust me – I know how much it hurts! Being dumped can knock your self-confidence beyond measure if you let it. So, do yourself a favour and be kind to yourself by looking at it as their loss instead. You may miss them, but they miss out on having you too, and sooner or later they'll realise *how amazing you are.* How foolish are they not to see your true value? Love yourself enough to save yourself for someone who appreciates you instead.

I want you to resist the temptation to hide away as a result of fearing embarrassment for having been rejected. The magic only happens when we open ourselves up enough to let someone in, but we always risk getting hurt. Nothing is ever certain. Just remember that you were brave enough to try, and – as the saying goes – if you want to win the lottery, you have to buy a ticket. Things don't always work out, but you must stay open to the possibility that it will, because this is the only way that it ever might. Tell yourself that you were bighearted enough to take a risk, and allow yourself to start to feel proud of your bruised heart.

You can't control someone else's decisions or actions. You can only control yourself and how you react. I get how hard this is to accept – I really do – but the sooner you accept this, the sooner you'll let go and move towards finding someone who appreciates your value. Don't beat yourself up. Sometimes things just aren't meant to work out. If you messed up, accept that you're human and learn from what went wrong, so that you can do things in a better way next time.

It's OK to give yourself a window of time every day to be sad, but then put it aside and try to get on with your day. To avoid spiralling into negative and self-destructive thoughts, it's a good idea to distract yourself by setting small, clear tasks to focus on. *Get busy*. Try to make yourself focus on something productive for a few hours in your day. A sense of achievement in small ways will help to level off your emotions. Write a to-do list of all those things that it's about time you got around to doing. Start by doing one thing at a time, so that you don't get overwhelmed. You'll still feel sad and will probably still cry. Don't expect too much of yourself. Just gently bring your attention back to what you want to achieve and keep going.

Find any opportunity to have a laugh, even if you don't feel like it; something funny can take you by surprise. Watch your favourite comedy series or stand-up comedian. It's amazing what having a good belly laugh out loud can do for your sense of perspective.

Keep away from sad songs, and instead listen to music with a strong and energetic beat.

Set yourself a deadline for your suffering. Make a pact with yourself that you'll be sad for a certain amount of time in weeks or months, depending on the severity of the situation. The general idea is that it takes half the length of the time you were in a relationship to heal, so if the relationship lasted six months, give yourself three months to get over it. During this time, aim to move yourself forwards every day with a simple, positive focus and by doing one thing you enjoy as a way to be kind to yourself. Then, visualise how you'll be ready to get on with your life again at the end of the sad time.

Give it time. Heartbreak is like having lacerations on your heart, and your heart doesn't heal instantly. Trust that it'll naturally heal itself if you let it be. Don't upset the wound by stalking on social media the person you've broken up with; make space and break all contact if you can. Getting involved with someone else too soon will only make you miss the first person more, so keep to your friends' company for now.

By shifting your focus to other things as much as you can, you'll allow the wound to heal by itself, and you'll eventually recover. You will regain your grounding, even though it may not feel that way right now.

Remind yourself of other times in the past when you've experienced other difficulties or upset, even if it isn't to the same degree. Remind yourself how you got through it then and how you did recover, even though you may have thought at the time that you never would. Although things may seem overwhelming just now, I want you to trust that you'll recover, and these simple steps will help you to do that one day at a time.

Notes:

How to cope when it feels all too much

If you're finding that your life right now feels all too pressured and too serious, it's likely that you're feeling the weight of demands on you. Maybe you're struggling with perfectionism or performance anxiety, because you're desperate to get things right, and are worrying what others might think if you get things wrong or you don't pull it off.

I'm here for you, and I want to give you as much hands-on help as I can, alongside this guide.

Action point: Make it happen!

You can get access to my free checklist *Ten Simple Strategies to Get You Through the Day* in the resources section at the back of the book. As a bonus, you'll also get access to my seven-day email series, with video content for extra support.

Inhale confidence - exhale self-doubt

FIND YOUR POWER!

Here are my specific snippets of advice to help you when you feel this way, so that you can be more chilled with your day:

» Don't get hung up on how you're doing something. Instead, let go, and allow yourself to just 'be' in the moment of doing it and to flow with whatever you're doing. Ironically, when you relax with it, you'll be less likely to make a mistake and do a better job overall.

» Do one thing at a time, and do that one thing slowly and deliberately. This will reduce stress and help you to enjoy the moment.

» Don't cram stuff into your day. Do less and give yourself time to absorb what you're doing more fully.

» When you're talking to your family or your friends, 'be present' with them. What I mean here is to pay attention just to them and to what they're saying, with no interruptions.

» Be firm with yourself and only acknowledge thoughts relating to the present time. Dismiss any past- or future-related thoughts, which may create stress for you. Keep bringing your attention back to the present moment.

- Allow yourself to become so absorbed in what you're doing that you lose yourself in the flow of that moment and just let time pass by. Have you ever had the experience of losing track of time? Do that more often. As your attention narrows, you become less aware of others and of yourself, which means you become naturally more confident and less self-conscious in that moment too!
- Most importantly, find the fun in your day today. Embrace it in the simplest of ways.

Be bold and let yourself go!

Notes:

How to overcome perfectionism

If you're motivated by the fear of not being enough in some way – in how you perform or in how you look – then the chances are that you may set yourself unrealistic expectations of perfectionism.

It's normal to feel out of control in some areas of your life, such as when things happen that aren't planned or expected. This throws you off balance. Striving for perfection is a means of controlling certain areas of your life excessively, because it feels like it compensates for those aspects you don't have control over. You're simply trying (albeit unhealthily) to find your way back to balance.

It's a good thing to have high standards and to set yourself personal goals to aim for. However, overly striving to meet these can create unrealistic expectations and overload you with unnecessary pressures. It makes it hard for you to hand your work in on time, show up on time, and be relaxed and confident in exams, and it can hold you back from trying out new things and living life.

Ironically, striving for perfection sometimes stops you from achieving success; it either makes you pull back because it all gets too overwhelming or you're constantly redoing things to make it right next time. On the outside, to your parents/guardians or teachers, you might come across as being lazy or lacking motivation because fear makes you procrastinate, being overly sensitive to criticism, being disorganised, being quiet, being over fussy, being unable to keep deadlines, or always being late. The truth is that, on the inside, you're feeling nervous, anxious, and consumed with the fear of not measuring up and failing.

FIND YOUR POWER!

The Serenity Prayer (see page 175) asks for us to accept the things we can't change, for us to find courage to change the things we can and for wisdom to know the difference. These wise words helped me to let go of perfectionism in my life. How would it be for you if you started to accept that you can't control the unexpected? Letting it go would mean that you could instead focus on what you can control, such as what you wear, what you say, what you do and what choices you make. Many teens I've helped have felt more relaxed and relieved as a result of accepting this challenge, because it helps you to begin to worry less.

When you're aiming for perfectionism, you'll tend to get caught up in 'black and white' thinking, which means things are either one way or the other, with no flexibility for something to lie in between: right or wrong, good or bad, or success or failure. To give yourself a break, start to challenge your thinking, and look for aspects of yourself or what you've done that are good. Help yourself by acknowledging that things are often not quite as bad as they seem.

Allow yourself to fail in small ways, and notice that the ceiling doesn't fall down! Learn from making small mistakes along the way, and you'll gradually begin to accept that not everything has to be right all the time, and you can still succeed. All mistakes help you to deepen your understanding and learn more, which – ultimately – fuels a greater achievement and bigger success. Reframe failure in this way, as a helpful means to get where you want to be.

Be sure to set yourself SMART goals; that is, goals that are Specific, Measurable, Achievable, Realistic and Time bound. Challenge yourself one small step at a time and acknowledge your achievements daily.

I want you to imagine that a little mini-me version of yourself is living inside your mind and driving your perfectionist behaviour. Imagine how tired she feels from constantly striving and cracking the whip. She has been trying to help you to feel safe, but it isn't working. It's just making you uptight and making her tired. Wouldn't she welcome a rest? Imagine you can talk to her and agree she'll ease up for a few weeks, so that you can trial a new way of thinking. This will be a new way to let go of the need to control what you can't, and to instead focus on what you can and make a difference there. Be sure to keep it realistic. You'll be glad you did. It made a huge difference in my life, and I know it can do the same for you.

Notes:

How to give your stress and worry away

Your mind is like a magnet for information, so it's easy for your mind to get *overloaded, overstimulated and overburdened by overthinking*. So now let's focus on letting go of any stress and negative thinking you may be holding onto, which is weighing you down, clouding your mind, and blocking your emotional and creative channels. You know, it's all that 'stuff' you carry at different times that depresses your mood and your energy.

FIND YOUR POWER!

It sounds a very simplistic idea, because it is – the best ideas are often the simplest.

So, here's how to do it:

» When you find that stress is getting to you, go outside for a walk. If it can be in amongst nature, where the air is clearest, then that's fantastic. If you're in a city, then maybe just try to find some streets that are a bit quieter, so as to escape from the hubbub of your busy day.

» As you walk along, think about what's troubling you, worrying you, frustrating you or even hurting you.

» Focus all your attention on this feeling of stress and begin to say to yourself, "This feeling… this feeling… this feeling…"

» Now imagine there's a ball within your mind, which – as it rolls through the pathways of your mind – is absorbing those feelings, along with all the information you don't need, and imprinting them onto the ball.

» Now, if you wish, imagine that you can take the ball out of your mind and into your hands. I wonder if it

feels light or heavy? You might like to release the ball directly from your mind by tossing your head as if you were heading a ball.

» Either way, now you can choose to throw the ball up to the universe and let the universe catch it. Breathe, lift up your hands and outstretch your arms.

» Now you can enjoy feeling lighter and clearer in your mind.

The physical action of throwing the ball up to the universe breaks the stress pattern of thinking negatively when experiencing that feeling and emphasises a sense of release. *Give this a try.* It might seem a bit whacky, but many of my students find it helps.

Notes:

Step 3

Learn to get along with others

Judge me
when you
are perfect

How to bully-proof yourself

Being bullied can make us feel isolated, inadequate and constantly on edge. It's a distraction from your studies, and can easily create intense feelings of being overwhelmed and not being able to cope.

I want you to know that a bully is someone who is secretly distressed. They are not happy with who they are, and they need to prove to themselves and the world, that they are significant and powerful enough. They want to rob you of your self-esteeem and self-confidence because they are feeling inadequate and suffering in some way. Being a bully means, they are simply directing their hurt and confusion onto someone else in an attempt to help them feel better; if they knock you down, they won't feel so lowly themselves. It's rarely personal to you, although I get that it totally seems it at the time.

If your self-esteem is a little shaky, you may be giving off a vibe that can make you susceptible to being bullied. When I was a child, I was bullied horribly at school in the first year of secondary education. I was already being bullied at home, and I carried that victim identity with me. Without even realising this, it was like I had hung a sign around my neck that said 'easy target'. My posture was closed and a little hunched, my voice was hesitant and I stammered over my words. Through my lack of confidence and low self-esteem, I was screaming out, "Come and bully me!" I didn't understand then that bullies target children who appear on edge, and who are unsure and insecure within themselves.

FIND YOUR POWER!

To help yourself to keep those bullies away, you'll need to learn to project an air of self-confidence and make sure your awareness is sharp.

Here's how to equip yourself with the skills to deflect bullies. These suggestions will help you to steer clear of this anxiety when you leave for school or college in the morning:

» Learn to walk tall, with your head up and eyes wide open. Bullies notice those who look down a lot and who are uncomfortable with making eye contact.

» Practise holding eye contact, because bullies will tend to steer clear of you if you look them straight in the eye.

» Identify areas where bullies tend to strike – this is often away from adult visibility. Locker rooms, toilets, corridors, and journeys to and from school are all hot spots. How might you keep yourself safer in these areas, so that you can avoid being alone and unseen?

» Your self-esteem is a measure of how lovable and likeable you feel. Your self-confidence feeds directly from growing your self-esteem. Who in your life loves and accepts you unconditionally? Ask them to

reinforce their love for you and to help you to understand that their love for you is unshakeable. You might like to ask them why they love you as they do, and if you could ever do anything to lose that love. When you understand their love more deeply, it may well help you to find your courage to rise to any challenge in a better way. This develops a belief in you that you are capable.

» Try to make many different friends. Invite your friends to spend time with you outside school or college. Whilst having just one good friend might seem all you need, when that friend is ill or away, you may feel lost and lose confidence. A loyal group of friends can be a fantastic force field against outside bullies. It also allows for flexibility in whom you choose to spend time with, as friendship dynamics change.

» Get into the habit of communicating confidently by speaking slowly and clearly.

» If you're lucky to live in a loving home environment, practise speaking up and saying how you feel at home. In that way, you'll find your courage to be assertive with your peers. Aggressive people who intimidate and shout lack the inner confidence to say how they feel calmly. Whereas, assertive people who communicate what's important to them have learned to be comfortable in defending themselves and their rights.

Notes:

How to handle being bullied by a friend or relative

We all need people in our lives in some way. Your life feels richer when you experience connections with friends and family. When you surround yourself with people who don't judge you and who love you for who you are, you grow to feel comfortable being yourself. Friends and family can be a real blessing that enriches your life in a supportive and loving way.

But what about those times when relationships don't work? When you feel bullied or manipulated?

You don't get to choose the family you're born into, and – at times – it might perhaps feel unacceptable to you to live with a certain relative's behaviour and their demands on you. Equally, friendships can deteriorate due to insecurities.

If you feel on edge around a certain friend or family member, it might be time to ask yourself some questions to help you to make sense of your relationship with that person. This will help you to glean what's really going on and determine what you can do to help yourself.

Is your friend or relative reeling you into their drama by creating drama in their life and in yours? It may be that, any time you confront him/her, he/she deflects the direct confrontation by going into meltdown, creating a huge argument, and he/she feels hugely offended by you. My guess is that you're left feeling frustrated and misunderstood, and still haven't resolved the issue.

Perhaps you feel manipulated by this person, which means that you feel you can't say no? They may use tears, fears or just push your buttons if they know you well enough to know what works on you. This is a seemingly clever tactic for them to get their own way, and not to compromise or give in to your needs.

If you feel uncomfortable, embarrassed or drained by this person, you're caught in a toxic and unhealthy relationship with them.

You need to take steps to safeguard your self-esteem and your wellbeing. Powerlessness creates anxiety.

"It takes a great deal of courage to stand up to your enemies... but even more to stand up to your friends."

– J. K. Rowling[1]

FIND YOUR POWER!

Here's how to help yourself break free from the clutches of a bully and hold onto your self-esteem:

- The best way is always to speak up about it to people you can trust. Bullies thrive on secrecy.
- Talking it through allows you to get some objective points of view, so that you can start to question whether the behaviour is, in fact, normal and acceptable, or not. It'll create some space for you to check in with yourself, and get clear about what you're prepared to tolerate and what behaviour is absolutely unacceptable.
- Find a means of communication between you and the person in question, either written or face-to-face, and make it clear that you'll *not* tolerate that behaviour. Reset the boundaries of your relationship and friendship.
- It may be that the person is actually unaware of the extent of their behaviour or the impact it has on you. Once you've made it clear how you feel, you may choose to give this person a chance to modify their actions. The reality is that you can't force someone to change their behaviour or to address, for themselves, their underlying need

to behave that way. If the person isn't willing to make a change, the only alternative is to create some distance between you and the relative, or to choose to find yourself a better friend.

» Get help to learn how to respect yourself enough. Take steps so that it feels totally unacceptable for anyone to dull your sparkle. Nurture your self-esteem and learn to give yourself permission to shine. When you do this, your energy will lift, and you'll no longer attract people who need to overpower you so that they feel less insecure.

Notes:

How to make friends easily

Starting out at a new school, college or university is both exciting and scary at the same time. When you don't feel great about yourself and you don't really believe you have much to offer, making new friends can stir up huge amounts of anxiety.

Everyone gives you the same old lame, non-specific advice, such as just to be yourself and you'll be fine, but – when your mind is already catastrophising that you'll be the only one without any friends, and that no one will ever be interested in you or want to partner with you for activities – the last thing it seems you would want to be is yourself!

The first thing to bear in mind is that everyone there feels the same. I want you to feel encouraged that you aren't the only one feeling anxious and unsure, and really hoping to make friends. So, hey, you already have something in common!

I've found it has helped me in my life simply to think of every stranger as a friend I haven't met yet. That way, I'm always open to the possibility of creating a connection with anyone new I meet.

It's a good idea to imagine what your perfect friend would be like in terms of personality, and what their interests and hobbies would be. By doing this, you'll help your mind to be alert to the right kinds of friends for you. Then, ask yourself, your family and your current friends what's great about you. Most of the time, other people see you more clearly than you see yourself, and you may well be overlooking some great qualities that make you a fantastic person to know.

FIND YOUR POWER!

It seems an obvious thing to say, but *be friendly*. Smile, and show kindness and consideration to everyone you meet. Don't try to be someone you're not, as people will see through it and won't trust you. Trust that there will be people who are drawn to your personality, just as you are.

The hard truth is that not everyone is meant to be your friend.

Not everyone will like you, but that's cool because you only need a handful of great friends. Quality wins over quantity every time! Rejection isn't something to fear – you reached out and it didn't work out. You didn't have that person as a friend before you reached out and you still don't. So, you're no worse off.

Don't make it about you. Move on.

Being brave and making the first move to talk to someone will be rewarded in most cases. Others will find you friendly and be grateful that you spoke first. Take every opportunity to talk to people around you: those who sit next to you, opposite you, in front of you and behind you. One of these people may well become your new best friend. Always be open to that possibility.

Look for opportunities to create connections. Practise some 'get to know you' questions that you can ask casually. Listen for shared interests and for indications that people feel the same way as you about some things.

When you're talking to someone, give them your full attention, listen carefully and make casual eye contact. They'll feel valued and like you more as a result.

Talk about your hobbies, and you'll discover people who share the same or similar hobbies. Talking about them will help you create a special bond, which may well develop into friendship.

Be prepared to stretch outside your comfort zone of what's familiar with your friendships, and get to know new people who are different to you. It'll help you to become more rounded as a person.

Get involved in extracurricular clubs and social groups. Encourage your new friends to introduce you to their friends. This will help you to build a network, not just of friends but of friends of friends too.

When you identify a potential friend, invite them to spend some one-on-one time with you. You can go deeper and get to know each other better when your attention isn't so diluted. You could perhaps study together or just chill together. It's a great idea to try out each other's different hobbies as a first experience too.

Be prepared for friendships to take time to grow. It doesn't happen overnight. It can take weeks to get to know someone, so be patient and stay positive.

Action point: Make it happen!

If you need help with some ideas to get new conversations flowing, I've created a list of twenty 'get to know you' questions to casually ask. *Twenty Questions To Get To Know Someone* is listed on the resources page at the back of the book. To access this right now, go to www.anxietybreakup.com/resources.

Notes:

How to avoid getting so worked up

When we forbid ourselves to feel, because it feels more comfortable that way in the short term, we aren't congruent (or in harmony) with ourselves, and this creates uneasiness within us physiologically – it throws us off balance. The more we hide our true expression, the more agitated we get, until something tips us over the edge and we explode. Have you ever noticed that, when you get really angry, it's not always that 'one thing' you're angry about, but it's about all the other unsaid stuff too?

Anger is a protective mechanism, which acts as a shield to mask hurt or pain. If you tend to lose your temper easily or if you feel yourself simmering like a pressure cooker waiting for the lid to blow, you may be 'nursing [or licking] your wounds'. At times, perhaps you choose to bury how you really feel about something for the sake of someone else's feelings or to keep things ticking along? Maybe you've learned to 'play safe', paint on a smile and pretend that you're OK. Possibly you just don't want to feel uncomfortable or make others feel that way around you.

As you were growing up, perhaps you learned that it wasn't safe to express yourself, that it's weak to show emotion, or that people won't like or accept you if you do? It's true that anger damages relationships, and makes others timid and wary around you. If you get angry often, you may begin to feel quite alone and misunderstood.

FIND YOUR POWER!

It's much healthier, mentally and physically, to learn effective ways to communicate how you feel, in a way that boosts your own self-respect and self-confidence. It earns you the respect of others too!

Learning to understand and express how you're feeling in a safe and steady way stops those sudden, uncontrollable explosions of anger.

So, next time you feel that stirring inside you, may I perhaps suggest that you take time to ask these questions – as you count to ten:

» What do I really want to say, but am afraid to? And why is that?

» What might happen if I do say how I really feel?

Above all, ask yourself what is the real consequence for you of not speaking your truth calmly and clearly, and of losing congruence with yourself?

Here's a simple frame of expression that doesn't create conflict, and that allows you to release your feelings in a safe and measured way.

» First, get in tune with how you're feeling, so that you own your feelings.

» Try saying to yourself, "I'm feeling [emotion] because [x] is happening, and what I really need right now is to [specific action you can take to feel more in control]."

For example, "I'm feeling irritated because Mum is nagging again, and what I really need right now is to leave the room so I can calm down."

Notes:

How to get them 'off your case'

How often do you switch off from demands because you're tired of feeling continually got at or nagged at? I myself remember how, as a teen, it can feel like you just can't do anything right. And what you do well goes unnoticed, right? I get that it can seem easier to withdraw and give up trying to get your point across. The problem this creates, though, is that people see you as just another sulky, uncommunicative teenager, and you lose respect.

Your parents/guardians, grandparents or teachers might suggest that you could do with developing a healthy respect for discipline. I can imagine how you might feel about such a comment!

As a teenager, you probably feel misunderstood and frustrated, because you're treated like a child but expected to act like an adult.

Here's how to help yourself when you don't feel heard. If you're a lot like me and feel how I used to feel, you'll feel more than just a bit isolated and misunderstood, and probably exhausted, if you're being barked at constantly. Do you ever say to yourself, "Why bother when they don't listen anyway?"

The hard truth is that this sense of rebellion you display, as a means to try to assert your independence and growing sense of identity, simply alienates you and gets you less of what you want.

So, how can you break this stand-off, so that you feel more satisfied, and can get back to enjoying being around your family and getting on better with your teachers?

Learning to communicate in a way that allows you to feel heard, lets you get your feelings, wants and needs understood in a way that doesn't create conflict. Trust me, I've helped so many teenagers to feel more empowered (and get more of what they and you want) by improving communication with their parents, in particular. Of all the tips and strategies I'm sharing with you here, this – without doubt – has the most power! (I certainly wish I'd known how to do this when I was your age.)

Effective communication is a win-win situation.

When you feel heard and understood, your resistance softens and the chances are that you'll be more willing to take on board others' requests of you. Do you agree?

Your actions earn respect.

What's more, by learning to communicate clearly and in a way that's non-confrontational, you'll earn respect for your actions too. Your parents and teachers will begin to view you differently, and this means they'll start to communicate with you on a more adult level, rather than talking to you as a child. So much conflict is created unnecessarily by parents talking to adolescents as if they're children, instead of the young adults they are.

Always remember that you have the power to influence how they treat you through the way you choose to communicate with them.

FIND YOUR POWER!

When you want to get your point across, always aim to talk first about how you feel, before you complain about whatever you may not be happy with.

Then state simply what you want or need them to do. Talking about how you feel first will get them listening, because you don't come across as whingeing or complaining. At the end of the day, your parent(s) or guardian(s) and many of your teachers care about your wellbeing, and they'll be interested to know how you feel.

Once you have their attention, you can let them know what you find irritating or frustrating. When you have their attention, it means they'll be more likely to take on board what you have to say when you then tell them what you want or need from them.

This is how to frame it:

"I feel [emotion] when you [specific action], and I really want you to [specific action you want them to do]."

Here are some good examples, which some of my teenage students have used in the past:

» "I feel frustrated when you don't give me a chance to explain, and I really want you to listen to my side of the story."

» "I feel angry when you yell at me, and I really want you to talk to me more calmly."

» "I feel annoyed when you moan about taking me somewhere, and I really want you to realise that I only ask you when I genuinely need your help."

» "I feel embarrassed when you kiss or hug me in public, and I really want you to save that affection for a less public place."

» "I feel irritated/overwhelmed when you nag at me to tidy my room, and I really want you to just ask me once or to remember that I'm under a lot of pressure with my projects."

Communicating in a clearer and more effective way will help you to feel understood and get more of what you want. You'll be subtly teaching the grown-ups around you how to talk to you in a more adult, more respectful and more considerate way too, so that's happy days!

Notes:

"You'll often hear people say, 'you're helping women find their voices'. I fundamentally disagree with that because women don't need to find a voice: they have a voice. They need to feel empowered to use it and people need to be encouraged to listen." – Meghan Markle[2]

How to be your own best friend

What would it mean for you in your world if you took steps today to learn how to really love yourself?

Just imagine what would happen in the world if everyone became a true best friend to themselves. What if people respected themselves enough to heal their pain, and to grow to honour and respect not just themselves but others too? Just think how many wars would be prevented, how many relationships and friendships would be saved, and how many children would grow up free from abuse. All these atrocities happen every day to good people, and are committed by people who are damaged, who are hurting and who need love. This is a mission that I bring to my work every day.

If you aren't loving yourself today, the ripple effect may well begin with you!

FIND YOUR POWER!

So, how can you take those vital steps, and learn to be kind and loving towards yourself?

Here's how:

- Accept yourself just as you are, with all your flaws and imperfections. Trust that you're doing the best you can with what you know, with how you feel and with the resources you have available to you just now.
- Don't beat yourself up with self-criticism and harsh words. Self-loathing might just be a bad habit you've picked up along the way. Ask yourself if you would treat your best friend or your pet the way you treat yourself.
- Pay attention to how you define yourself. 'I am...' is one of the most powerful phrases you'll ever use. If you describe yourself in a negative way, you're weaving your words into your identity. So make sure that the phrase you use is positive and encouraging. Ensure that you focus on what you want to be and feel, and not on what you're not, nor how bad you feel.

» Realise that it's actually OK to love yourself. Give yourself permission to learn how to do this. A recent student who was suffering from very low self-esteem commented that she had grown up absorbing a belief from her father that it's not good to love yourself, and that if you love yourself and let your light shine, you're playing to your ego and you become vain. She had learned his religious interpretation that it was un-Godly to love yourself! We're not talking vanity here – that's the extreme, and it's conceit borne from insecurity. No, here, we're talking about befriending yourself and learning to trust in yourself enough to speak the truth about yourself. You can choose to speak your truth to yourself by using positive, encouraging self-talk and to speak to others in a quietly confident way.

» Try to imagine a clone of you, and how this clone can be your best friend, loyal and loving, and who just wants the best for you. Doesn't this clone of you deserve to be loved in return? Imagine the kind words you would choose to say to the clone of you who is within you.

Notes:

Step 4

Learn to feel good about yourself

"I can't think of any better representation of beauty, than someone who is unafraid to be herself."
– Emma Stone

How to quit pretending and be honest

Have you ever agonised over making a phone call, meeting someone, sending a message or posting on social media? Do you go over conversations in your head and worry whether you made the right impression?

But what happens when you're not yourself? When my self-confidence was low, I used to try my hardest to behave in the right way to help myself to fit in more or to be the 'right person'. I'm guessing this is something you do too, right? The thing is, when you do this, not only does it create a false impression of who you are but you also lose your naturalness. The irony is that it creates the very thing you're trying to avoid, because people instinctively pull back from you. You don't come across as your true self, and they detect a lack of honesty and transparency. You sense it from them immediately, don't you? Then, you start to feel anxious, and ask yourself questions such as these: "What did I do?", "Why are they pulling away?", "What's wrong with me?" and "Why can't I get this right?"

It can feel as if your self-talk is on steroids. Perhaps you find that, when you work hard at trying to get it right in terms of what you say and what you do, you get caught up in overanalysing? The simple truth is that living as if you have 'something to live up to' can be a major factor in the levels of anxiety you experience. It can be just exhausting trying to impress everyone and have everyone like you!

You can relax when you are yourself. For you, fitting into a box or a framework of boundaries by playing someone else keeps you caught up in overthinking, preoccupied by your own self-talk (or internal dialogue) and missing opportunities to connect with other people. Maybe you're already questioning this for yourself? How might it benefit you and those you spend time with to show up as yourself?

Do yourself a favour and quit pretending!

I used to be so hung up on what other people thought of me, personally and professionally. It was such a relief to grow to understand that people are so hung up on trying to make an impression themselves, that they just need you to be yourself!

Have you ever considered that the people you pretend to are pretending right back at you? Isn't it time you did yourself and them the favour of being honest?

FIND YOUR POWER!

Can you imagine how connected to you someone will feel if they have your full permission to quit pretending and relax, and for them to just be themselves? Anxiety just melts away.

Getting other people to trust you comes from honesty, and this isn't just from honesty towards them but from being honest with yourself. You can take steps today to learn how to understand yourself and your own vulnerabilities, to love yourself, and to trust yourself. When you do this, you'll find your courage just to be yourself and smash anxiety.

Here's how:

» Don't run from your emotions. Instead, tune into how you feel about something or someone. If you're cross, be cross; if you're scared, be scared; and if you're feeling bored, be bored!

» Don't push aside your feelings about what you want or shrink inside so that others feel more comfortable. Instead, give yourself permission to own your feelings, and to calmly voice your opinions and ideas. Always remember that if someone holds a different opinion to you, it doesn't make your opinion wrong (or theirs!) – it just means you see it differently, and that's OK.

» As you learn to be true to your feelings, in turn, you'll become truer to who you are. This means you'll naturally feel more confident, because you'll grow to understand your core values and what makes you 'you'. You'll squash the fear that you won't be good enough if you are yourself.

The truth is that the more genuine you come across, the more others will respect and like you.

Notes:

How to be true to who you are

I want you to imagine that your life is like a story book – a story of you. Let's call it your *Book of Me*. What's the story you choose to tell yourself today?

Every day, you write another page in your *Book of Me*. This is your story and the chronicle of your life. Every day up until now, you've lived your life based on a story you may not even be aware exists. This story creates a blueprint of beliefs and expectations.

As you've grown, you've been expected to live and behave in line with this story. Trouble comes when this story doesn't fit with who you feel you are and who you want to be. You may find yourself living someone else's story. You may feel guilt and shame, and you may feel pressured to conform and fit in by those close to you.

This conflict – the battle between what you want, and either what you're expected to do/have or how you're expected to be; or the battle between your heart and your head – feels like anxiety.

Now is the perfect opportunity for you to begin a new chapter in your *Book of Me* – perhaps to begin to think about writing your own story in a way that feels truer to you?

When you live your true story and allow yourself to become who you want to be, you will find your true self, find your way to ease stress and become happy.

FIND YOUR POWER!

Here's how you can make a start today. Think about those times in the past when you tried to change something and to branch out, but when it felt so uncomfortable that you gave in, and slipped back inside that familiar and safe comfort zone of discontent.

What dream did you dare to dream that got squashed?

Identify what you wanted but didn't get at that time. What were the pressures/expectations of others that made it difficult? What was the belief within you that pulled you back? In what way did you doubt yourself? Your belief is written in the blueprint of who you've become; it's a bit like a script that tells the story of who you are. Any doubt tugs you back inside that story and keeps you stuck in your life right now. You simply can't perform beyond that story. You have to write an updated version for yourself within your mind, and live that story instead.

Realise that, when you give in to those doubts, you may not be being true to yourself. Instead, you're most likely reacting to those pressures and expectations: the 'musts' and 'shoulds' you hear. This can negatively affect your self-esteem, because you start to believe that you can't trust yourself to override

those 'musts' and 'shoulds' in order to make your life different and better – and it makes it harder for you to try again.

Although it might not seem like it, I want you to know that you do have a choice. Acknowledge that you do. You really don't have to stay bound to someone else's expectations of you. Instead, give yourself permission to create strong affirmations to remind yourself of the truth about you, and what you truly want and need to be happy.

Begin to imagine and dare to dream it. Visualise just how you want yourself to be. Make this picture as vivid and real as you can. Aim to capture the emotion of this moment as if it's real right now, and you'll send a compelling message to your subconscious mind. You'll begin to write your own story.

Notes:

You are
powerful,
beautiful,
brilliant
and brave

How to be confident with sex for the first time

Like everything, sex doesn't start out being amazing! Sexual confidence and pleasure come with experience over time. First sex is an unknown, and – for so many reasons – most of the time the idea of having first sex creates anxiety. It's really important to manage your expectations to keep yourself from feeling overwhelmingly pressured. It's somehow assumed that you'll just know what to do and how to do it, which adds way too much pressure.

It's so normal to feel conflicted. On the one hand, you may be curious, and want to enjoy the physical and emotional pleasure of sex, but – on the other – you may be afraid of getting hurt physically and emotionally too. The magic of sex happens when you and another person grow trust between you, and you both feel safe to be vulnerable and to explore together.

Sex can feel like a minefield, as you perhaps begin to experiment with the different sides of sex which are more than simply penetration, such as masturbation, 'sexting', phone sex, sending sexy pictures and oral sex – and then there's being brave enough to admit that you're not even wanting to have sex yet.

Over time, as you grow more sexually confident, sex becomes more enjoyable and you feel more body confident too.

Sex and masturbation are in no way dirty, or things to be ashamed of or embarrassed about. Your parents grew up mostly with outdated stigmas and judgement around sex, which can – in some cases – make it hard for them to talk to you openly and freely.

FIND YOUR POWER!

You can help yourself to feel more comfortable and empowered with first sex if you take some time now to question for yourself what might feel right and what might feel wrong to you before it actually happens.

Sex must only happen when both people have no doubts whatsoever that they definitely want it to happen.

No always means no!

If you're around people who are doing lots of bragging or sex talk, it can make you feel like you're the one getting left behind, when the truth is that – in reality – this may not be the case. If you rush into something you're not ready for, just to keep up, the chances are that it may not go well and you'll regret that you did. So, give yourself permission to take it at your pace and trust your intuition.

Sex should never feel manipulative. Feeling pressured to have sex because you might lose someone if you don't will leave you disrespecting yourself and feeling disrespected.

I want you to think of your body as if it's a temple of sacred treasure. You have total power over whom you share your body with. So, only share it with someone

who totally appreciates the privilege of sharing in the beauty of you!

Only ever having safe sex will mean you can focus on the pleasure of intimacy and have fun with it, without fear of pregnancy or infection.

Get to know you and your body for yourself. The more you grow to understand what turns you on and turns you off, the more it'll help you to feel confident to express yourself during sex. That way, you'll get the most enjoyment out of it.

Cuddling together releases the hormone oxytocin. You need to know that this feel-good, 'love' hormone creates a bond and gets feelings flowing. The more you cuddle, the closer to each other you tend to feel, and the more likely you are to fall in love and risk heartbreak. Sex without cuddling can be less emotionally tied. If you want to pace staying in control of your feelings, limit the amount of cuddling.

Lastly, I want you to always be mindful that alcohol can affect your judgement when it comes to having sex. It can mean that sex might happen when it wouldn't otherwise, because alcohol lowers your inhibitions and affects your judgement at times too. It can affect your decision-making and how well you're able to communicate your wishes. To get the most of out of your early sexual experiences, it's worth limiting your alcohol intake for sure!

'Comparanoia' – the fast track to anxiety

'Comparanoia' is a made-up word (from combining 'compare' and 'paranoia'), which summarises so well the anxiety that's created by comparing yourself to others. We can easily become paranoid that we're simply not good enough!

Do you ever get hung up on what other people think of you? When you don't feel great about yourself, it's easy to assume that others are judging you harshly and that they see what you're choosing to see in yourself. That just makes you feel a whole lot worse, because you're validating your belief that you're not a good person to know, you're not capable and so on. Perhaps you feel yourself shrink more inside yourself, which gives others even more reason to judge you, right?

Of course, the flip side of this is that you see *them* as damn near perfect – they're just so confident, so happy, so set up in their life and things are just so rosy for them. When you do this, you can't help but lose out.

Consider this. I've learned that if you're going to compare, then you might as well compare everything. Being human means we all have flaws and no one's life is as rosy as it seems from the outside. On the surface of things, it's true you might not be as good in some way, so you'll lose a nugget of self-esteem, so to speak. But if you dig deeper and compare more, you'll find things you're better at, and then you might win some nuggets back too!

FIND YOUR POWER!

When you compare, make it fair.

Be a friend to yourself by focusing on what's good about you and telling the truth to yourself. Turn it into a game for yourself, and find a reason every day to acknowledge something good that you've done or a quality you've noticed in yourself. Consider all those many things that you can be grateful for in your life if you only choose to look.

This way, when you go to compare yourself with others, you'll be better placed to catch yourself in the act of assassinating your self-esteem and, instead, will be able to choose to remind yourself of what's good about you. So, you might say something such as, "OK, so I'm not as successful in my studies as she is, but I'm blessed with a family I adore"; "I don't have a loving, supportive mum in my life, but I have fantastic friends"; or "She is a much better tennis player than me, but I can swim really well."

Something else that's worthwhile is to let yourself just stay with the feeling that comparing yourself with others creates in you – and turn jealousy into a positive desire to achieve that quality the other person has, and get curious. I wonder if there's an opportunity for you to develop in yourself a quality or a skill that the other person already possesses? Choose to see an opportunity to compare yourself with others as a way for you to question how you might choose to grow. Get to know the people you're comparing yourself with more. We only become bitter when we give in to the powerlessness that arises from thinking we have a raw deal and that we can't change it – but that's just a belief, isn't it?

Notes:

How to keep your mind healthy

Many years ago, a wonderful mentor and trainer, Greg Forde, made the following comment. It made a huge impression on me at the time and has stayed with me.

"Your mind is like a pot of fertile soil. Your thoughts are the seeds. You grow flowers or weeds."

When you were born, your mind was just like a pot of fertile soil: pure, rich, well fed and eager to grow something – you!

A little seed can germinate and grow into beautiful flowers, but it also might grow into unhealthy weeds. Life can blow seeds through the air into that pot from other plant life nearby, which can influence what grows there. Bugs and worms find their way to that pot too. Before you know it, the pot of waiting fertile soil is alive with activity.

If you tend to the pot well, you'll encourage the bugs to leave.

Sow the right seeds, nourish and water them, and let some light shine on them, and you'll get pretty flowers to enjoy.

Do you tend to criticise yourself, talk badly or gossip about others, and always expect the worst? Perhaps you feel guilty or ashamed about something, or maybe you resent certain people or your situation? In this way, you're growing weeds, which become anxiety and, eventually, depression.

So, how can you root out those weeds in your thinking, and create a prettier and healthier perspective on your world?

In addition to the power points listed in the next section, as an extra bonus for you I have a free special workbook to guide you, step by step, through a unique strategy that will help you to smash any beliefs that are holding you back just now.

Action point: Make it happen!

My *7-Step Strategy to Smash Limiting Beliefs* is listed on the resources page at the back of the book, but to access this right now the link is www.anxietybreakup.com/resources.

FIND YOUR POWER!

Recognise that your life is a mirror of your thoughts, so if you're thinking negatively, you'll continue to find yourself in negative situations and you'll attract people of a similar negative mindset to you. They say we're a product of the five people we spend most of our time with, so take a look around you – are you living amongst weeds?

Decide today to catch any negative thought as if you're digging over your pot of soil and tossing out any weeds you don't want, which don't serve you. As soon as you notice yourself saying something negative out loud or inside your head in self-talk, just imagine uprooting and tossing out an ugly weed. In its place, plant the seed of a positive, encouraging and loving thought instead – if you get stuck with this, the easiest way to do this is to say to yourself the complete opposite of what you were thinking.

Here are some suggestions of how you might flip negative to positive thinking:

» If you're thinking something like "I'm such a failure!", instead say, "I'm really good at some things; I can do this. I just need to take my time and figure it out."

» If you're thinking something like "I'm so fat!", instead say, "I'm already

looking slimmer. Choosing to look after my body, making healthy food choices and getting active really works."

» If you're thinking something like "I can't cope. This is too much!", instead say, "I'm finding this difficult today, but I can handle it."

» If someone tells you "You're wrong!", instead say, "It's not that I'm wrong, we just see it differently."

You'll quickly learn to catch yourself as you get into the habit of thinking more positively about things, and the weeds will jump out at you, just like they do in a garden that's well tended and stocked with flowers. Keep on weeding!

Notes:

"We are all born
so beautiful.
The greatest tragedy
is being convinced
we're not."
– Rupi Kaur

How to feel better about your body

Learning to love and accept how you look is the absolute best thing you can do for yourself! It goes hand in hand with learning to believe in yourself.

Society might have you believe that it's arrogant to accept and appreciate how you look, but this is simply not true. Rather than having a poor body image seeming modest, it's actually damaging to your self-confidence and seeps into every part of your life. Learning to love and accept yourself just as you are will help you to feel happier and more at ease in every way.

It's easy to be influenced by the media, with its vast amounts of fashion or gossip-column images of seemingly perfect bodies, most of which have been tweaked by Photoshop or smart phone image apps. Marketing is all about selling a feeling, and advertising wants you to believe that – whatever your body shape – you'll look and feel better when you buy a particular product, regardless of whether you consider yourself thin, fat, ugly, too tall, too short or whatever!

The truth is that you're already OK without their product.

Avoid conversations that focus superficially on how someone looks. Help yourself to hold a more rounded perspective. Instead, direct the conversation with your friends to talk about other aspects of yourselves, such as energy levels, health and fitness, or entertainment. It's mostly our energy and vitality that determines how attractive we seem, rather than the physical features that determine how we look.

FIND YOUR POWER!

Challenge yourself to start to appreciate the different parts of your body and focus on the function of each, rather than how it may seem to you physically. Look at yourself in the mirror (naked if you can!) and talk to each part of your body in turn, saying how you're grateful for the job that part of your body does. For example, say, "Thank you, nose, for helping me to smell every day." Really imagine how your body wouldn't function the same without that part. Then, challenge yourself to say, "I love you, nose." Notice what thoughts come up for you. Hear how you criticise yourself. Practise catching the thought and overriding it with a more helpful, kind thought instead. This sounds daft, I know, but it helps you to shift your perspective and learn to accept all parts of you more fairly. Get into the habit of stroking and touching your body softly in a loving way. How do you touch someone you love and care about? Learn to touch and hold yourself in the same way.

As a second mirror exercise, look over your whole body, notice where your attention sits critically and then find something else that you choose to think better of instead.

This is how it works. Start at your face and be honest with where your attention goes – right to any aspect of yourself that

you don't like. Notice that you're focusing negatively. What you focus on will grow to become an even bigger issue for you. So, challenge yourself to look beyond what you don't like to something about yourself that you may be overlooking. For example, instead of focusing on your big forehead, choose to lower your gaze and notice what's lovely about your eyes. Every time you look in the mirror, choose to focus on your eyes and tell yourself something nice. Seeing a fault in your forehead, for example, is just a bad habit. Create a kinder habit, and you'll start to feel better about yourself. If you need help, ask a trusted friend to tell you your good points as they see you.

As the Serenity Prayer (see page 175) says, you must learn to accept what you can't change and change the things you can. You can apply this to how you feel about your body. If you're not happy with your body image, in shape or size, what can you do to improve this? Be honest with yourself about your eating habits or how you exercise. Learning to love your body means taking care of your body and appreciating it for the temple that it is, which houses your soul. We only get one body. Isn't it worth learning how to love and value it? After all, it goes with you everywhere you go!

I hope this has helped you to realise that it's possible for you to shift perspective if you choose to look at things in a different way.

Step 5

Learn to believe in yourself

"I don't like to gamble. But if there's one thing I'm willing to bet on, it's myself."
– Beyoncé

How to let your inner confidence shine

When you were born, you were overflowing with confidence and self-love. You totally believed that you deserved attention and adoration, and you screamed and demanded that your needs were met. Over time, other people may have found it difficult to meet your demands and your needs, and – due to their own inadequacies and insecurities – they may have begun to criticise, and withhold affection and attention. Maybe they even hurt you. They may not have realised the damaging effects of their actions, but you may have begun to withdraw gradually, to protect yourself. Human nature means we're naturally egocentric, and always assume that there's something wrong with us, or that we did something wrong or bad. Maybe this happened to you, and you began to doubt yourself and to hide a part of you away, because it felt safer that way?

Living life with low confidence means you hold yourself back and you stop yourself from participating fully in life, so you don't feel fulfilled. I totally get that it can feel safer and easier to just peek out from behind the curtain now and again. But wouldn't you secretly rather draw back that curtain, hear the drum roll or the orchestra play, and walk confidently and self-assuredly onto the stage of your life?

FIND YOUR POWER!

If this is true for you, as it once was for me, here's what helped me; I hope it does the same for you:

1. **Think yourself confident.** Your thoughts, feelings and behaviour are inextricably linked, so – by changing your posture and your body language – you can help yourself to feel and think more confidently. Walk tall, keep your head up and smile. With open gestures, eye contact and an upright stance, you'll lift your energy and you'll come across as being more confident, and it'll help to actually grow your confidence too.

2. **Take pride in your appearance** – in the way you dress, your hair, your nails and your shoes. When you go out to any social event, make sure your clothes and shoes fit properly, so that you feel comfortable, you can walk properly, and you aren't worried about your top gaping or your tummy bulging. When you feel good about your self-image, you'll naturally feel more confident and comfortable being noticed.

3. **Slow your speech.** Do you ever babble on when you're not feeling confident? When you slow your speech, you can breathe more easily and be clear on what you want to say.

Because you're speaking more slowly, other people will understand you and will listen more intently. This will, in turn, help you to feel listened to and that what you're saying is of value, which will boost your confidence and help you to relax.

4. **Watch your self-talk.** Practise catching and cancelling any negative self-criticism or negative perspective on your day. Immediately flip it around to a lighter, opposite perspective. Decide to look on the positive side and be kind to yourself. Be enthusiastic in finding solutions instead of dwelling on any problems.
5. **Compliment yourself,** and you'll soon be feeling comfortable about accepting compliments from others. Give yourself permission to notice what you do right and to acknowledge the positive qualities you hold that enrich the daily lives of others. Create a list of affirmations (positive statements that begin with "I am"), which evidence these things. Remind yourself of these often, and this will help you to feel better about yourself. You'll like yourself more, and it'll boost your self-esteem.
6. **Take stock of who you spend your time with.** Whom do you listen to? Who influences you? Consider your friends and family. Create space for yourself, either temporarily or permanently, away from those people in your life who put you down, deflate you, criticise you and generally make you feel bad about yourself. Choose to spend your time with people who boost your energy and your mood, and who support and encourage you emotionally.

7. **Set yourself small, achievable goals every day.** Choose to support and encourage yourself to achieve these goals in baby steps, and acknowledge the progress you make.

Your confidence is there within you, hidden from view, and these strategies will help you to shine a light on your confidence, so that you can set yourself free to enjoy more fun in your life.

It won't happen overnight, but if you trust yourself and 'keep on keeping on' every day, you'll get there. I did, and so can you.

Notes:

A square peg in a round hole - the anxiety of not fitting in

Do you ever feel socially that you're a square peg in a round hole? So many students over the years have used this expression to explain their feelings of social anxiety to me.

Feeling this way means you've told yourself that you just don't fit in and there's nothing you can do, so you remain an outsider at most social occasions, looking in on everyone else having a good time.

But here's hope: being an 'inferior' square peg is an illusion that your thoughts have created.

Somehow, you've learned that it wasn't OK to be yourself, and that – in order to fit in – you had to be the same or similar to everyone else. This is simply not true. We humans crave individuality – just imagine how dull friendships would be if we were all a clone of each other.

You're right not to sacrifice your authenticity so that you're seen to fit in. Be proud to be yourself.

"Don't feel stupid if you
don't like what everyone
else pretends to love."
– Emma Watson

FIND YOUR POWER!

Here are some ideas to help you get comfortable socially:

1. **Pay attention to your self-talk.** In what way might you be thinking negatively about yourself and about other people? Might your thinking be restricting you in connecting with others?

   Quit telling yourself that no one likes you or that you don't fit in. Instead, choose to think about what you want from the social occasion in question, the kind of people you want to meet and what you would like to do. Seek out these people and do more of these things.

2. **Make the effort first.** Being anxious socially, you might have got into the habit of hanging back and waiting for the others to talk to you first. Be bold and start talking. Start with saying, "Hello," and then keep talking!

3. **Turn your focus away from yourself.** To keep from spiralling into destructive self-talk, turn your attention away from yourself and move it onto the person you're talking to. Be interested. Keep eye contact, smile and ask questions. When you acknowledge other people's individuality, it becomes easier for you to share yours too.

4. **Forget approval.** When you worry too much about what people think of you, you tend to seek their approval so that you can feel comfortable in their company. You lose yourself when you do this, because your focus is on what they want and not what matters to you. Instead, make it OK for you to worry about this less and do more of what you want to do, just for you.
5. **Take steps to heal any past hurts or current stresses,** so that your energy is more welcoming, and less protective or suspicious of others. In this way, you'll attract more positive people into your life.
6. **Take the time to get to know yourself.** In what particular situations and with which particular people do you feel most uncomfortable? Consider honestly what you like and appreciate about yourself, and find out what others – whose opinion you value – see in you. Others reflect to us what we often don't accept in ourselves. Growing to respect and accept yourself more means you'll be less critical and more open towards others.
7. **Everyone feels a bit awkward sometimes.** Notice who else might be feeling uncomfortable, and go and talk to them. You'll have something in common, at least, which may forge a connection, and the chances are that you'll both relax a little more and begin to chat naturally.
8. **Don't try to fit into established cliques** – it's likely you never will. So, decide to make your own instead, with people you feel comfortable enough around to be yourself.

Notes:

Five easy steps to overcome social anxiety

When your self-talk is louder than the conversation, you don't hear!

Walking along a canal in East London one morning, I began to notice how everyone amongst the many joggers, walkers and cyclists avoided eye contact, preferring to stay disconnected in their own isolation.

I want you to know that the biggest hurdle to overcoming social anxiety is keeping yourself disconnected from others. When you avoid connection with others, you validate a belief that there's something to fear in reaching out to others, and social anxiety grips you deeper.

Without help, social anxiety can easily spiral out of control. I helped a girl on the tube in London recently, who had got herself so worked up on her way somewhere social that she had a panic attack in the carriage. I don't want this to happen to you, so I have a bighearted offer for you.

Action point: Make it happen!

You can equip yourself really well to manage panic attacks and keep them away with my special programme, which guides you through the key strategies, and – because you've bought this book – you can buy it at a special discounted price. What's more, it's supported by an MP3 audio file to make it even easier for you to use. Check out *How to End Panic Attacks* in the resources section at the back of the book. You can get started right now through this link: www.anxietybreakup.com/resources.

It's easy to feel alone, especially in any big city. When you're full of self-doubt socially, even the smallest place feels like the loneliest place on earth. Endless hours of disconnection every day reinforces your sense of isolation and makes it harder for you to connect with others at times when you want to.

FIND YOUR POWER!

If you're looking to overcome social anxiety, follow these five simple steps:

1. Challenge yourself today and make eye contact with someone.
2. Then challenge yourself further and smile.
3. Ask someone for the time.
4. Ask another for directions, even if you know where you're going.
5. Go and order a coffee, or buy something in a local store, and pick something random to comment on to the server, so that you initiate a brief, safe conversation.

Do this a few times in your day every day, and – by the end of the week – I guarantee you'll be feeling more confident within yourself, less alone and more connected within your community.

You'll be on your way to giving social anxiety the boot for good!

Fate whispered to the warrior,
"You cannot withstand the storm..."
And the warrior whispered back,
"I am the storm!"

How to overcome the fear of failure

If you fear failing, you're certainly not alone! As a teen, you're entering the most exciting time of your life, which is filled with endless opportunities and possibilities to take your life in many different directions. I get how overwhelming that can feel. Perhaps, at times, you feel completely stuck, and unable to make a decision for fear of making the wrong choice or for fear of not being good enough at what you do.

The questions "What if it doesn't work out?" and "What if I fail?" keep you caught up in worrying about the consequences of a wrong decision. Your imagining of all those possible negative future outcomes stops you from taking responsibility and action in the present.

The reality is that any decision worth taking involves some risk of failure. With so much advice thrust upon you, and so many people telling you what to do, it's absolutely vital that you stay true to yourself and to your values. What's the pressure you feel under? And where's it coming from? Is it the expectations of others who have influence over you, or are you perhaps placing unrealistic demands on yourself?

As you've grown up, what have you learned from your parents about failing? Failure must not be judged as inadequacy or weakness; it's merely an opportunity to learn and grow. It means you haven't mastered a particular skill yet. Asking yourself, "What do I need to learn to achieve this in the future?" helps you grow. Sometimes, when things don't work out, it's simply an indication that you need to change direction.

FIND YOUR POWER!

Get comfortable being uncomfortable. What feelings surface for you when you fail? Learn to get comfortable with uncomfortable feelings such as embarrassment, sadness, guilt and anger. When you worry less about coping with these feelings, you'll fear failure less.

"Fail to plan and you plan to fail" is a very true saying! Make sure you prepare well in advance for any exam, project or presentation, and you'll hugely increase your chances of success. It'll help to calm your nerves too, because you'll know you've already put the work in to learn what you needed to learn, so that you can deliver.

Get confident in how you'll cope. Dare to go to the worst-case scenario of failing if you put yourself out there, and identify what it is you're most afraid of. Challenge your fears by working out how you'll cope if it goes wrong by telling yourself, "So what if 'x' happens, I'll do 'xyz'."

Do it for you. In what way might you be seeking approval by trying to meet others' expectations? Why does it matter so much what they think of you? If you feel your parents' or guardians' love or approval hangs on what you do, rather than who you are, I'd urge you to question them about this – the chances are that you may be pleasantly mistaken.

Give yourself a break. Work on accepting yourself fully for who you are, with all your faults and inadequacies alongside your strengths and your talents. Every human is imperfect and fallible. You're no different.

Cultivate friendships and relationships that are encouraging, loving and supportive. Surround yourself with positive feedback, and you'll find it easier to practise healthy self-talk.

Define what success means for you. For every challenge you set yourself, define at the outset what success will look like, so that you'll recognise it when you get there. Focus more on the fun of learning new things and new skills along the way, rather than just the final outcome. Be sure to acknowledge your effort and incremental achievements. This will help you to nurture your self-worth along the way, even if you don't get the final outcome you want.

Learn from those who have failed before you. Take the time to ask people you respect about how they've failed in their lives at times and then recovered to achieve success later on. What did they learn along the way? And how did they better themselves as a result?

Research how some famous people failed at first, but then achieved great success. This will motivate you to remember that failure is often part of the journey to success.

Notes:

"If you're always trying to be normal, you will never know how amazing you can be." – Maya Angelou

How to trust yourself in tough times

There's a beautiful, strong and bold beech tree in my garden, near to one of my consulting rooms. It stands proud and tall. Its trunk is thick, and its roots go deeply down into the soil. No storm can move it; it stands firm against all the elements. I've watched this tree during the strongest winds in the darkest nights, as the branches sway and the leaves rustle, but the solid trunk of this mighty tree simply doesn't move.

When we have a wobble in our lives and struggle with anxiety, we have forgotten that we can be like that tree.

It has helped me in past stormy times to think of myself with the strength of that tree inside. Life can sometimes whip up a storm, and knowing how to stabilise yourself when the storm hits can make the difference in how and, indeed, whether you weather it and survive.

You must grow to trust yourself; to challenge any storm with an equal or greater power from within.

FIND YOUR POWER!

Remind yourself of the most challenging times in your life so far that you thought you wouldn't be able to handle.

You're stronger than you know!

What was it that got you through those tough times? Consider each situation and how you handled it. What actions did you take? What did you believe about yourself or the situation that pulled you through it? It's vital that you bank the evidence for yourself in terms of how you handled it. You'll remind yourself of just how strong and capable you really are.

You owe it to yourself to nurture strength and certainty within you, so you feel reassured that – when life whips up an unexpected storm – you're able to trust your inner warrior to stand strong, and ground yourself deep using your roots, just like that beautiful, old tree in my garden.

How to stretch and grow

How often do you give yourself credit for doing the best you can with what you know and what's available to you just now? Being hard on yourself is a hard habit to break, I know.

It's easy to buy into the idea of a quick fix for anxiety. The trouble with such an offer is that if it doesn't work for you, it eats away at your self-esteem – you'll feel worse within yourself, which feeds anxiety.

It's easy to buy into the idea of a quick-fix technique or a promise of help, but then you'll likely find that it doesn't quite work for you in the way you had hoped. When you take steps to work on yourself, you'll experience shifts and moments of enlightenment, but – in truth – there's no quick fix. We're all a work in progress, which is ongoing. When you're willing to make a commitment to yourself to gently and consistently take the right action to understand yourself and allow yourself to grow in your life, that's where the magic is!

FIND YOUR POWER!

Your *key steps to personal growth* are as follows:

- **You have to really want it!** Take some time to *consider the impact* of the cost of staying stuck where you are, and how healing yourself and your situation will positively impact you and those you love. Be prepared to invest well in yourself to get the best help available to you.
- **You must understand and accept that there will be resistance to change.** Your mind will always steer away from the unknown and try to pull you back to what you know. To grow, you must challenge this and be prepared to consistently stretch beyond your comfort zone into your 'stretch zone'. Taking action in small steps within your stretch zone will keep you growing. If you find yourself in the 'panic zone', you've simply taken too big a step forwards before you're ready. You clearly need to make the step smaller and then try moving forwards again. Growing is never comfortable, so you must get comfortable being uncomfortable. Help yourself to stay in your stretch zone for a good amount of time every day, and talk to yourself encouragingly.

» **You must own your problems and own your commitment to creating a life that works for you.** It's vital that you're willing to invest in quality help and support to guide you, but – above all else – you must be willing to engage and actively follow the steps to make transformation happen.

» **We all have safety mechanisms, which keep us caught up in rigid and inflexible thinking at times.** Are you always right? Keep an open mind, and you'll allow yourself to be open to the possibility of seeing things in a different way and taking a different course of action.

» **You must be willing to take small risks within your stretch zone in order to grow.** Doing things in a different way and trying new things on for size *is* a risk, but not taking that risk may be the biggest risk of all for you!

» **You must be open to learning about yourself.** Perhaps you've learned to stay inside your head when you deal with issues. To grow, you'll need to learn, not just intellectually from your headspace but also to understand and trust your emotions, so that you learn from your heart-space too.

» **You must be willing to develop awareness for yourself of how you're getting in your own way.** You may be holding on tight to beliefs and behaviours you don't want, because there may be a hidden benefit that you haven't considered or owned up to yet.

I always remember a comment made by a school friend when I was wanting to change my situation. A throwaway line, but one I've never forgotten! She said this:

"At the end of the day, if you want something badly enough, you'll get it, and if you don't, you didn't want it as badly as you thought you did!"

I urge you to ask yourself every day how badly you want to be rid of the anxiety in your life. Consistent, steady action will get you there, one step at a time.

Notes:

Next Steps

Unleash your inner warrior

What matters most is what you do next

I really hope you understand how entirely possible it is for you to take control and change things for the better, using the strategies in this fast-track guide. You bought this book (or it was given to you) for a reason. Don't let that reason fade away and go to waste. With this book, you've got everything you need to know to get you started, but without action nothing will change for you. Developing trust and confidence in yourself is an active process. You already have within you everything you need to make it happen.

It's now time for you to step out of the shadows that have kept you playing small in a victim identity and mindset. I urge you to follow my lead and find your own warrior within.

Rise up and fight back using your feminine energy!

You don't need masculine aggression to be assertive within yourself or about yourself. You just need to allow yourself to recognise the power in your vulnerability, and use this energy to surge forwards. Accepting your own vulnerability doesn't mean you're a victim. It doesn't make you weak. You only become a victim when you give in and take no action to get yourself out of the situation you're in. When you take action, it'll make you more powerful than you ever thought possible.

Your journey to freedom starts now. It's your time to step up, take your place on life's stage and own it!

Always remember that we all have the resources within ourselves to be amazing. Just because life throws you a curve ball at times and makes you forget, it doesn't mean your power isn't there.

I hope this book has helped to remind you of just how awesome you truly are. The power is already within you. Don't fear the storm. Join with me and celebrate your inner warrior. You've got this! I know you can do it. You've come this far with me, and I don't want you to stop now.

So, tell me, what's the first step you can take today to begin to break up with anxiety for good? What will you decide to put into practice every day that will make the difference for you?

I'd love to hear how you're getting on and how this fast-track guide has helped you. I would strongly suggest that you retake the *anxiety quiz* at regular intervals as you put these strategies into practice, so that you can monitor the progress you're making. It would make my day if you would share your thoughts on Instagram using the hashtag #anxietybreakup or email me at gethelp@anxietybreakup.com

Following this section, I've included a resources section for you that lists all the downloads and support I've mentioned throughout this book.

Resources

Free Resources

All of the resources detailed in the Warrior Action Points can be accessed here: **www.anxietybreakup.com/resources**

Resources to Buy

Offered at a special discounted price for those who have purchased this book. (Enter code BOOK50)

» *How to End Panic Attacks*

» *5-Step Plan to Calm a Panic Attack*

» *3-Step Strategy to Keep Panic Attacks Away*

» *MP3 audio file – Overcome Panic Attacks*

Link to purchase at www.anxietybreakup.com/resources

Working with Me Directly

Six-Week Online Mentoring Course

On the resources page (www.anxietybreakup.com/resources), you'll find details of my mentoring course especially for students, with hands-on support and weekly Q&A, which dives deeper into strategies to help you further develop your confidence. Find out more today!

Talk to Me

Just because you've reached the end of the book, please don't feel you're on your own with this. I'm here to help you going forwards. If you would like an informal chat with me to explore how you can continue to grow your confidence, I'd love to hear from you. Simply send me an email, and we'll schedule a time to talk that suits us both.

Follow me on Instagram (@anxietywobbles) for more self-help tips and advice.

To find out how to work with me one to one, either online or in person, and/or to read my monthly blog on a range of topics related to anxiety, please visit my website or contact me directly.

Website: https://lisaskeffington.com
Contact me: gethelp@anxietybreakup.com
Freephone 0800 6890981

References

Page 91

1. Rowling, J.K. (2001). Harry Potter and the Philosopher's Stone. London, UK: Bloomsbury Publishing, P. 221.

Page 107

2. Furness, H. (2018). Meghan Markle says women 'don't need help to find their voice' as she urges Royals to harness Time's Up and Me Too campaigns. The Telegraph, [online] 28th February. Available at: https://www.telegraph.co.uk/news/2018/02/28/meghan-markle-excited-joins-harry-william-kate-set-royal-charitable/ [Accessed 28 February 2018].

Page 177

3. Woman & Home (2018). 50 Amazing Women Over 50 Awards. Woman & Home, June 2018, P. 57. Shortlisted in category, 'Shaping the Future'.

The Serenity Prayer

God grant us the serenity to accept the things we cannot change,

the courage to change the things we can,

and the wisdom to know the difference.

- Reinhold Neibuhr (1892-1971)

My Story

Until my late 20s, I struggled with anxiety. I was underweight. I stammered over my words. I had digestive troubles and horrendous skin problems; I was plagued with acne and cold sores. I was bullied at home and bullied at school. I was crushed to the point that I even suffered nervous convulsions! Life was just horrid. I felt so alone and so misunderstood. I didn't like who I was, and I had no confidence in myself at all. It was simply that I wanted the craziness within me and around me to stop! But I felt powerless to make that happen.

At 17, with help, I began to understand how I had surrounded myself within a wall of limiting self-belief, because my confidence was smashed, and I was caught up in believing – because I had been told so often by an obsessively controlling father – that I knew nothing, that I was no one, and no one would ever love me or want me.

I worked hard, and with the help of some amazing teachers at Longfield School in Kent, at 18, I got myself away and off to work in London, and then on to Barcelona to study and work.

I had convinced myself I had it sorted. I told myself, "I did get away and on with my life, after all," but inside I felt lost, and I was insecure, angry, defensive and quaking, with buried anxieties.

It took an emotional breakdown, years later, for me to finally find the right help to break up with anxiety and put my past behind me. I've never looked back.

I began to understand and accept myself truly for the first time in my life; I began to break free from the anxiety that had kept me down in a place in the world that wasn't meant for me.

I began to understand for myself what doesn't work when battling anxiety and what really does. As I began to find the answers that would help me to genuinely believe in myself and to break free from those limiting self-beliefs, I grew to understand myself and to accept myself for the first time.

The aim of this book is to teach you the shortcuts for you to create the right mindset and to set the right boundaries, so that you can find your way quickly to loving yourself and creating a life that works for you on many levels, whatever your circumstances are right now. I hope this book helps you on your way to feeling free, happy, relaxed and secure within yourself for the rest of your life.

You can read my full story at www.lisaskeffington.com/AboutMe.

Described as "the helper for anxious teens" by *Woman & Home* magazine,[3] Lisa was honoured to be shortlisted in the '50 Amazing Women Over 50 Awards, 2018 for her contribution to 'Shaping the Future', through her dedication to helping teenagers who have anxiety and emotional stress, and helping their families.

Student Success Stories

What others have said about how I've helped them

Here are some comments from young women who have followed my advice. Their identities have been changed to provide anonymity, but the comments themselves are entirely in their own words.

"I felt anxious about how my parents viewed me and I was worried I wasn't making them proud. Now things are amazing. Everything with my parents is so much better and I don't worry about many things any more."– Abigail, 14

"I was suffering anxiety in everyday situations,feeling overwhelmed and unable to cope in general. I was comparing myself to others, self-conscious and holding myself back in performance. I feel so much more confident and positive and able to do anything I want to do. I'm worrying much less about what other people think of me. I'm not feeling as tense about things like giving presentations at school and asking questions."– Becky 15

"I needed help with anxiety and to build my confidence. I was panicking about tiny issues, not believing in myself and making everything harder than it had to be. Now I have more confidence with my friends and I can handle any difficulties with my studies much better."– Anastasia, 16

"I was struggling with confidence and feeling anxious about starting a sixth form college. Things are really good now. I have loads of friendship groups and I find it easier to talk to people." – Chloe, 16

"My confidence is back and I've settled really well into Uni life. I've made friends and am happy and totally comfortable living away." – Katy, 18

"I had been feeling really overwhelmed and anxious in my Uni studies and having difficulties in some friendships. I have really settled into my new course and am feeling really confident about my future at Uni."– Monica, 19

"I was struggling with confidence in myself, and being over anxious about things. Now I have learned to identify and counter any negative or anxious thoughts. I have noticed that this has definitely improved my moods and made me feel a lot more positive about my future. I feel a lot more relaxed and happy about things and within myself."– Emilia, 21

"The idea of meeting new people paralysed me. I overthought how they would view me. It kept me from meeting anyone new. I didn't want to put myself out there and try out new things or speak up at Uni. I have definitely become more confident. I can chat freely to more people without overthinking. I actually get excited to meet new people now. I've joined societies at Uni and I feel more confident with my decisions academically. I had defined myself before as an anxious person but now I've realised I can go outside my comfort zone and talk to new people, which is fun." – Trudy, 22